The Paradox of Progressivism,
and Other Essays on U. S. History

J. M. Beach

West by Southwest Press
Austin, TX

West by Southwest Press
Austin, TX

Table of Contents

5

The Paradox of Progressivism,
and Other Essays on U. S. History

I

A Nation Divided:
Understanding Our Culture Wars
A Historiography of American Nationalism

Introduction:
The Institutionalization of a Debate

America is still in the midst of a culture war. Many see America deeply divided and polarized by ethnicity and race, by moral values, by political parties, by class, by gender, and by a host of other variables. Public discourse in America ranges from vitriolic partisan denunciations to diplomatic relativism to scholarly argumentation to ignorance and apathy. Is there a path that will lead beyond this culture war? In order to address that question Americans first need to understand the root of the conflict. Fundamentally, the disagreement is over national identity: What is America, and who is an American? To understand this fundamental conflict one must listen to and embrace a heated debate in order to outline a diverse array of answers. But in order to outline a schematic of American nationalism, one must understand the origins of the American nation and its complex trajectory through history. In looking to American history one must ask: Are there antecedents to our current cultural war? Have there been older disagreements over American national identity?

If one examines the historical record, especially outside the boundaries of traditionally defined political authority, dissent and discord pervade American identity. According to the founding document announcing the birth of the American nation, "The Declaration of Independence," "all men" were "created equal" and had certain "inalienable rights" given to them by their "creator." Among the most important of these rights were "life," "liberty," "the pursuit of happiness," and the right to a responsive representative government that would protect the people's rights, as well as their "safety and happiness." But even before this hallowed political document would be approved by the Continental Congress and announced to the world, the wife of one Congressman, Abigail Adams, wrote to her husband on March 31, 1776 and scolded him and his fellow American congressmen for being hypocritical. How could these men proclaim "liberty," inalienable political rights, and the "emancipation of nations" while they were depriving women of their liberty and rights. She pointed out to her husband that American men did not truly know what liberty or equality meant because their idea of liberty and equality were only for a privileged, male few. Abigail warned that women would not take the "tyranny" of men for long and they would rebel, free themselves, "subdue" their masters, and then "without violence throw both your natural and legal authority at our feet."[1]

And yet the assertive Abigail Adams was only willing to extend her critique so far. Just a year earlier she had written to her husband about the fearful "conspiracy of the Negroes," by which she meant those slaves who had the audacity to petition for freedom in return for fighting along side the English against the insurrectionary colonists. Abigail apparently could not understand why black slaves wanted their freedom just as much as she did, nor could she understand that these blacks would do whatever they could to attain their liberty – including fighting against the hypocritical Americans (as Abigail herself threatened) whose "liberty" and "equality" where mainly for propertied, white men.[2] The black American David Walker would later address the American republic in 1829, "Do you understand your own language? Hear your language proclaimed to the world on July 4th 1776 – 'We hold these truths to be self-evident – that ALL men are created EQUAL!!'" In 1850 Frederick Douglass asked, "What, to the Slave, Is the Fourth of July" – "This Fourth of July is *yours*, not *mine*."[3]

At the same time that diverse participants of the American nation were contesting the very meaning of America, there was also a solid tradition of self-assured Americans (ironically, many of them immigrants) trying to consolidate a single, unified vision of America. Not long after the revolution propagandists like J. Hector St. John De Crevecoeur praised the "modern" American nation as everything backward Europe was not. Crevecoeur claimed the original English settlers were "enlightened" as they "discovered," "settled," "embellished," and laid the foundation for what would become America. He also claimed that this new modern nation was being developed by and for white, Northwest Europeans who were busy creating "a new race of men" – "the American, this new man." But to become American these Northwest Europeans ("English, Scotch, Irish, French, Dutch, Germans and Swedes") had to not only leave behind their old culture, language, and customs, but also "embrace" the new American government and culture, which just so happened to be a highly Anglicized culture infused with Protestant and capitalist values.[4]

---

[1] Abigail Adams, "Letter to John Adams 31 March 1776" & "Letter to John Adams 7 May 1776," in *The Letters of John and Abigail Adams*, Frank Shuffelton, ed. (New York: Penguin Books, 2004): 147-49, 168. For John Adams reply to Abigail see "Letter to Abigail Adams 14 April 1776" (154).
[2] Mia Bay, "See Your Declaration Americans!!! Abolitionism, Americanism, and the Revolutionary Tradition in Free Black Politics." In *Americanism: New Perspectives on the History of an Ideal*, ed. Michael Kazin and Joseph A. McCartin (Chapel Hill, NC: The University of North Carolina Press, 2006): 25-52.
[3] Mia Bay, "See Your Declaration Americans!!!, Ibid.
[4] De Crevecoeur, J. Hector St. John, "Letter III: What is an American," in *Letters from an American Farmer*, Susan Manning, ed. (1782; reprint, Oxford: Oxford University Press, 1997): 40-82.

By 1811 the Anglo-Protestant John Quincy Adams could confidently write his father, "The whole continent of North America appears to be destined by Divine Providence to be peopled by one nation, speaking one language, professing one general system of religious and political principles." Of course the "one nation" that Adams foresaw was a white man's nation, a Protestant Christian nation, a capitalist nation, and these convictions would lead many white men to proclaim a new self-evident truth. The *Democratic Review* on July 1850 announced, "The fact that the dark races are utterly incapable of attaining to that intellectual superiority which marks the white race is too evident to be disputed." It was a simple extension of deductive logic to thereby conclude, as did James De Bow in *De Bow's Review* in 1854: "The Negro till the end of time will still be a Negro, and the Indian still an Indian. Cultivation and association with the superior race produce only injury to the inferior one. Their part in this mysterious world-drama has been played, and, like the Individual, the race must cease to exist."[5] But of course this drive for cultural unity, racial purity, and national solidarity as a white man's nation was contested all the way. Elizabeth Cady Stanton addressed the New York State Legislature in 1860 and let them know that the "white Saxon man['s]" ridiculous "prejudice" against "color" and "sex" were not congruent with "The Declaration of Independence." She declared sarcastically that "negroes" and women were not "monsters" and thus they too deserved liberty and political rights. She wanted the nation to remove all the prejudicial legislation against women and blacks and then to "strike the words 'white male' from all your constitutions."[6]

This essay is an attempt to outline a historical schematic leading up to our late 20th/early 21st century culture war in order to historically contextualize our current debate within a much larger and older debate over American national identity. The central focus of this essay is the debate: a longstanding and contested deliberation over national identity and purpose. This essay will not and cannot bring any resolution to this debate; however, this essay will try to clarify the basic structure of the debate and attempt to historically contextualize it. The basic thesis that this essay will argue and demonstrate is that the democratic nation of America was founded on an irresolvable debate. It was and is a debate, to quote the historian Joseph J. Ellis, which "was not resolved so much as

---

[5] Reginald Horsman, *Race and Manifest Destiny: The Origins of American Racial Anglo-Saxonism* (Cambridge, MA: Harvard University Press, 1981).
[6] Elizabeth Cady Stanton, *Address to the Legislature of New-York, Adopted by the State Woman's Rights Convention, Held at Albany, Tuesday and Wednesday, February 14 and 15, 1854* in *The Norton Anthology: Literature by Women, The Tradition in English,* 2nd ed., Sandra M. Gilbert and Susan Gubar, eds. (1854; reprint, New York: W. W. Norton, 1996):466-68.

built into the fabric of our national identity. If that means the United States is founded on a contradiction, then so be it."[7] The United States of America was consecrated on debate and its foundational documents, the Constitution, the Bill of Rights, and the Declaration of Independence, all were designed to protect and project that debate into the future – the American nation can be seen as the institutionalization of a heated, contradictory, often ugly, sometimes democratic, yet always deadly serious debate. Our 21st century culture wars are an important testament to the longstanding tradition that defines and unties the American people: the constitutional imperative to freely speak, debate, and at times fight over[8] the identity and direction of the American nation. Issues, parties, perils, crises, and credos come and go, but the debate over our American identity continues to define who we *all* really are, have been, and will be. It is our inheritance – both a promise and a curse. America is dying! Long live America!

---

[7] Joseph J. Ellis, *Founding Brothers: The Revolutionary Generation* (New York: Vintage, 2000): 16.

[8] In the *Declaration of Independence* Jefferson clearly declared the right of Americans to "alter" or "abolish" any government that did not represent and protect the people's natural rights. While not explicitly advocating violence, any abolishment of an existing institution would arguably necessitate force or violence of some kind, and thus, forcibly defending one's rights is arguably a right of the people. This statement seems to thereby justify and institutionally consecrate the right of political violence directed at securing and protecting other natural rights.

Conservative Reaction
to 20th Century Liberal Reforms

The conservative reaction to the liberal state, the rights movements of the 1960s, and the general unrest caused by counter-cultural uprisings was varied in temper, scope and accuracy. Many right wing polemics expressed only anger, condemnation, and righteous rage. Some mixed nostalgic fantasies with biased readings of the recent changes initiated in the 1960s. A few articles and books articulated reasonable claims backed with evidence in an attempt to put forth a scholarly argument for conservative policies. All conservative reactions were defensive as they implicitly or explicitly tried to uphold a particular conception of a unified and monocultural Anglo-Protestant based America, which they saw being damaged or destroyed by the legacies of the 1960s. Despite claims made by many dismissive liberal nationalists,"[9] conservative defenders of a distinctly WASP America abound, and they have became arguably more vocal, more impassioned, and under the reign of George W. Bush, more empowered. However, it must be added that conservative arguments or rants for a monocultural America have been extremely repetitive in their uniform allegiance to a mythic golden age of WASP American glory, civic virtue, and harmony.

Allen Bloom's *The Closing of the American Mind* (1987) was perhaps one of the most important early salvos of reactionary conservative critics. Bloom's "meditation on the state of our souls" was an angry conservative manifesto disguised as a metaphysical treaty on human nature, truth, and the classical virtues of a "liberal" education. The problem, as Bloom saw it, was a shift in cultural priorities and values, which had infected the classical "liberal" curriculum and was "indoctrinating" students to see "wars, persecutions, slavery, xenophobia, racism, and chauvinism" around every hallowed corner of Western history. The new "open" curriculum lacked refinement and cultured discrimination because it accepted "all kinds of men, all kinds of life-styles, all ideologies." It was nothing like the "old" American curriculum, built on an established liberal arts tradition, which taught refined students to "recognize and accept man's natural rights" and the "fundamental basis of unity and sameness" that had been recently discarded by divisive liberal cant like "class, race, religion, national

---

[9] David A. Hollinger claimed that "virtually no one defends monoculturalism." David A. Hollinger, *Postethnic America: Beyond Multiculturalism* (1995; reprinted & expanded, New York: Basic Books, 2005): 80.

origin, or culture." Bloom was very concerned that American students, and the country in general, were loosing sight of the "natural human good" and the refined ability to "admire it when found" (like the traditional "heroes" of American history). Bloom thought that a revolution had taken place whereby "minorities" had "assaulted" and "weakened" "the sense of superiority of the dominant majority" (WASPs) in order to destroy the old older and set up relativistic "nation of minorities and groups each following its own belief and inclinations" in stead of following the traditional and objective "common good," which was disappearing in a wave of relativistic "conformism:" it was the closing of the American mind.[10]

Bloom wanted to remind Americans that "culture is a cave" and every human being is raised within a particular traditionally defined "cave" in order to be inculcated into the "standards" that make us a "culture-being;" however, culture is limiting and keeps humans from the light of "nature" and "truth." Western "science," derived from the ancient Greek search for truth, is the only way to escape the Platonic cave of culture into the wider, permanent truth that is the "rational quest for the good life according to nature." The current dogma of cultural relativism teaches "openness" to the "closedness" of cultural caves, which lock students in ethnocentric bias of cultural fallacies. According to Bloom, the traditions of Western science and the liberal arts (embedded and preserved in American culture) contain the superior and universal human truths that all "men" need to escape their limited cultural caves in order to gain the eternal and universal truth of the human condition: "The active presence of a tradition in a man's soul gives him a resource against the ephemeral."[11]

The Civil Rights movements of the 1960s had "dismantled" the "structure of rational inquiry" and "ideologized" the student population with "whatever intense passion moved the masses." But Bloom warned his audience, "The nation was not ready for great changes." The rush for social change only "radicalized" and "politicized" education, and the new heretical cry of "racist" was shouted irrationally from every campus at decent bastions of the old order. Bloom was quite dismayed and claimed, "so far as universities are concerned, I know of nothing positive coming from [the 1960s]; it was an unmitigated disaster;" it was a "crime." The "old core curriculum" was dismantled and destroyed and replaced by a vapid "egalitarian self-satisfaction" that amounted to "nothing." The 1960s was the "source of the collapse of the entire American educational structure" because "the knowledge of philosophy, history and literature" was "trashed," and replaced with "dogmatic answers and trivial tracts."

---

[10] Allen Bloom, *The Closing of the American Mind* (New York: Touchstone, 1987): 19, 26-27, 30-31.
[11] Bloom, Ibid., 36, 38-39, 247.

The new dogma was derived from a "new moralism" (actually an older "antimorality"), which put forth the quasi-goods of "modern democratic thought:" "equality, freedom, peace, cosmopolitanism." Lost in this democratic vulgarity were traditional social goods, like the "natural differences" of human beings, the "restraints" of liberty, the glories of war, and patriotic "devotion to family or country." In fact, this new democratic dogma concealed a "covert elitism" that actively "suppressed" the "superiority" of certain peoples, especially rulers, in order to patronize the "ambition" of average commoners. It also ignored the plain facts that certain races are superior to others.[12] Bloom was quite clear in his assertion of American exceptionalism: "America tells one story: the unbroken, ineluctable progress of freedom and equality;" and now "is the American moment in world history...the fate of freedom in the world has devolved upon our regime." However, based on the cultural and political changes of the 1960s, America's ability to seize its privileged destiny was in "doubt."[13]

Another important conservative reaction was *Cultural Literacy* (1988) by E. D. Hirsch, Jr. Hirsch's tone was much more subdued and scholarly then Bloom's, and Hirsch restricted his reaction to the subject of literacy and its central importance to a democracy. Hirsch admitted that "flux" permeates culture, but that "stability not change" should be the educator's primary obligation to the young and, thus, "cultural literacy" should be the primary object of education: "the persistent, stable elements belong at the educational core." The primary purpose of schooling is to "acculturate" children into "our national life," which Hirsch assumed to be a "shared culture." But later in the book Hirsch asked a telling question, "Shall we aim for the gradual assimilation of all into one national culture, or shall we honor and preserve the diverse cultures implicit in our hyphenations?" Hirsch was able to admit the legitimacy of the "vocabulary of a pluralistic nation" and say, "American national culture is neither coherent nor monolithic, and no convincing attempt fully to define its character has ever appeared" and so he argues that the U.S. educational endeavour should be guided by a "value-neutral" "vocabulary." Of course this raises the question about whether a "value-neutral" vocabulary or educational project is even possible. But Hirsch's call for "neutrality" was disingenuous because he actually intended to promote a "conservative" "means of communication" so as to acculturate students into a "traditional culture." He tried to defend his policy by

---

[12] "The fact is that the average black student's achievements do not equal those of the average white student in the good universities, and everybody knows it. It is also a fact that the university degree of a black student is also tainted, and employers look on it with suspicion, or become guilty accomplices in the toleration of incompetence (96). Bloom stated flatly: blacks are "manifestly unqualified and unprepared" for good universities (94).

[13] Bloom, Ibid., 313-15, 318, 320-22, 326, 329, 55, 97, 382.

stating, "Traditional information by no means indoctrinates [students] in a conservative point of view," and that "teaching children national mainstream culture doesn't mean forcing them to accept its values uncritically." However, it is hard to see how the whole educative endeavour under the "primary and fundamental" direction of the "acculturative responsibility" to "teach the way's of one's own community" cannot avoid using the soft-power of cultural hegemony. What safeguards do children have within the public schools when bureaucratic or professional functionaries fall back on a rigidly defined national curriculum and simply indoctrinate children so as to satisfy the predominant public good, which Hirsch believed at the time to be meeting "the needs of the wider economy."[14]

While Hirsch is certainly more reasonable and reasoned than Bloom in his conservative arguments for a common culture and nationalist education, his position still boils down to conventional wisdom and traditionalist assumptions, bottoming out on the bedrock of preferring (without explaining or systematically arguing for) one set of values over another:

> Although nationalism may be regrettable in some of its world-wide political effects, a mastery of national culture is essential to mastery of the standard language in every modern nation. This point is important for educational policy, because educators often stress the virtues of multicultural education. Such study is indeed valuable in itself; it inculcates tolerance and provides a perspective on our own traditions and values. But however laudable it is, it should not be the primary focus of national education. It should not be allowed to supplant or interfere with our schools' responsibility to ensure our children's mastery of American literate culture. The acculturative responsibility of the schools is primary and fundamental. To teach the ways of one's own community has always been and still remains the essence of the education of our children.[15]

If "American national culture is neither coherent nor monolithic," as Hirsch noted earlier, then how could he uphold abstract platitudes as "our own traditions and values," while also admitting that communities have their own ways, which should be taught? Whose community or interests

---

[14] E. D. Hirsch, Jr., *Cultural Literacy: What Every American Needs to Know* (1987; reprinted, New York: Vintage, 1988): 12, 29, 110, xvii, 95, 102, 23, 24, 18, 73.
[15] Ibid., 18.

should be taught and who in the community should decide? What *part* of the diverse community decides the issue? Hirsch's arguments seem to advocate a curriculum based on a unified and singular "national" U.S. culture, but the question then arises what exactly is a national culture, and is it ever a unified collection of clearly defined interests based on the desires of all parties involved? Whose culture, whose nation, whose values, whose world-view will dominate and declare "our own traditions and values" as the uniform standard? Hirsch does not address these questions and seemingly takes it for granted, as did Bloom, that *his* national culture is the "common culture," and thus the only national culture that should be taught.

In "Americanization and the Schools" (1999), E. D. Hirsch argued that Americanization should be a common function of the public schools for all children, immigrant and native alike.[16] He also said that "ethnic identity" does not necessarily have "to be sacrificed in the course of Americanization," but he did not explain how this can be avoided. He emphasized that "failure to master the nuanced use of English in speech and writing places a severe limit in the United States on one's opportunity, and freedom, and the amount of money in one's purse...Those Americans who lack effective mastery of English, including mastery of the shared background knowledge that enables its nuanced use, are destined to stay poor and alienated from mainstream social and political life." Hirsch dismissed charges of "cultural and linguistic imperialism" because he viewed a shared language and culture as a "universal" practice and a "social necessity." Everyone needed to be Americanized according to Hirsch: "New citizens and citizens-to-be deserve the same Americanization as other American children. All American children need to be Americanized in a deeper sense...This system of common knowledge and root attitudes needs to be imparted in school not just to achieve a citizenry competent to rule itself, but also to achieve community, social peace, and, not least, economic justice." Hirsch invoked Horace Mann and argued for Americanization through a "common curriculum" that would articulate an Americanization program that would *not* be a "narrow, nationalist indoctrination" but a "special universalist sentiment appropriate to a nation of nations:" Patriotism, claimed Hirsch, "implies love of country without implying hostility to the other...American patriotism is built of shared knowledge, attitudes, loyalties, and values – including values of non-exclusion and toleration." The "need for a common language is the key to a trans-ethnic future." Hirsch attacked "bilingual movement" and the "multicultural movement" as "education sisters" that articulate a program of "romantic

---

[16] E. D. Hirsch Jr., "Americanization and the Schools," *The Clearing House* 72:3 (Jan/Feb, 1999): 136-39.

particularism," which he decried as the "mortal enemy" of "Enlightenment cosmopolitanism." He also claims that these movements have "deepen[ed] the disadvantage" of "unassimilated" children and thus they helped "preserve the economic status quo and even widen the gap between rich and poor." Hirsch argued that "militant bilingualism and multiculturalism" have made the schools "even more confused and rudderless places than they had already been."

Another important conservative barrage, and perhaps the most important and significant conservative argument of the 1990s, came from noted liberal historian Arthur M. Schlesinger, Jr. and his bestselling political tract, *The Disuniting of America: Reflections on a Multicultural Society* (1991, 1998). Schlesinger made a concession to the liberal camp and argued, "cultural pluralism is a necessity in an ethnically diversified society" such as the U.S., however, his book was an extended argument for a conservative common culture based on WASP values. One line of argument invoked Hirsch and explained that a "common language" is an "essential bond of cohesion in so heterogeneous a nation as America." The other, more important line of argument focused on the "democratic principles" of America which he enveloped in a teleological grand narrative: American political history was the "persistent movement" from "exclusion" to "inclusion," "openness," and "tolerance." However, he did make a nod to critics on the left by admitting that American principles have "too often" been "transgressed in practice" due to Anglo-American "domination" of "culture and politics" and WASP "convictions of racial superiority."[17]

Schlesinger admitted that traditional U.S. history has been "invoked to justify the ruling class" composed of "white Anglo-Saxon Protestant males" who conceptualized American history to serve their own distinct "interests." However, Schlesinger did not linger on this point or find it necessary to condemn. Instead he argued that Americans must embrace their past, "for better or worse," and come to terms with the WASP tradition as the cultural foundation of America.

> The smelting pot thus had, unmistakably and inescapably, an Anglocentric flavor. For better or worse, the white Anglo-Saxon Protestant tradition was for two centuries – and in crucial respects still is – the dominant influence on American culture and society. This tradition provided the standard to which other immigrant nationalities were expected to conform, the matrix into which they would be assimilated.

---

[17] Arthur M. Schlesinger, Jr., *The Disuniting of America: Reflections on a Multicultural Society*, revised ed. (1991; revised, New York: W. W. Norton, 1998):80, 115, 142, 123, 19, 54.

Schlesinger used this conception of a foundational common culture to explain how it has become more inclusive because of the grand narrative of progress unfolding in U.S. history. He quoted the conservative historian of education Diane Ravitch who said, "Paradoxical though it may seem, the United States has a common culture that is multicultural." The point he developed was that even though the WASP culture was a dominative and self-seeking culture that forced other peoples to conform to its standard, it was a self-critical culture, a culture defined by democratic principles, and above all else, it was a culture that was willing and able to "forge a single nation from people of remarkably diverse racial, religious, and ethnic origins." American culture may be based on the foundation of an older WASP culture, but that WASP culture was able to facilitate "progress" towards a "new national identity:"

> *E pluribus unum*: one out of many. The United States had a brilliant solution for the inherent fragility, the inherent combustibility, of a multiethnic society: the creation of a brand-new national identity by individuals who, in forsaking old loyalties and joining to make new lives, melted away ethnic differences – a national identity that absorbs and transcends the diverse ethnicities

The "brilliant solution" of the melting pot, which leads to a "new American culture," was never fully documented or explained by Schlesinger, and his argument is complicated and confused as he admitted that many ethnic groups were skeptical of the melting pot solution, especially considering the centuries of xenophobia, white supremicism, and racism that has only recently been "acknowledge[d] and confront[ed]." Schlesinger noted how many minority groups throughout American history had to "demand" their political rights through "declarations of ethnic identity," which gave rise in the 20th century to "ethnic politics" and has culminated in the denunciation of melting pot theory as nothing but "a conspiracy to homogenize America." Instead of documenting and reconciling this melting-pot debate, however, Schlesinger rushed to a hasty and simple conclusion: a "new *American* culture" has been produced through the unfolding of historical progress, culminating in the Civil Rights amendment, but petty "cults" of ethnicity have mushroomed from the 20th century Civil Rights struggle. These ethnic cults "threaten to become a counter-revolution" and could destroy the hard-earned new national identity. These ethnic cults must conform to the "common American nationality" because America was, is, and must continue to be "'one people,' a common culture, a single nation,"[18]

---

[18] Ibid., 158, 34, 144, 132, 17, 46, 34, 142-47, 49.

By the presidential election race of 1992 the rhetoric of the culture war was being used by the radical and religious right. In order to scare up political support, conservative reactionaries took the debate to new levels of aggressiveness. Patrick J. Buchanan led a campaign for the presidency on the extreme political and religious right, but he eventually came back into the mainstream Republican fold to support George Bush. At the 1992 Republican National Convention he railed against liberals and the "failed liberalism of the 1960s and 70s" as the arbiters "of doom." It was the noble Republican, Ronald Reagan, who returned American to the "Judeo-Christian values and beliefs upon which this nation was built" and he "made us proud to be Americans again." Energized by eight years of a powerful Republican administration, religious and social conservatives loudly proclaimed that the socio-political change of the 1960s and 70s were "not the kind of change America wants. It is not the kind of change America needs. And it is not the kind of change we can tolerate in a nation that we still call God's country." Buchanan argued that a "religious war" was being waged in America over "the soul of America:" "It is about who we are. It is about what we believe. It is about what we stand for as Americas…It is a cultural war." Buchanan called for a new conservative movement that would use "force, rooted in justice, backed by courage" in order to "take back our culture, and take back our country."[19] Two months later, Buchanan expanded on this same theme and delivered another speech, "The Cultural War for the Soul of America" (1992). Buchanan was indignant over charges of his "divisive," "hateful," and "racist" speeches, and he thundered, "As polarized as we have ever been, we Americans are locked in a cultural war for the soul of our country." He quoted a newspaper columnist and explained, "It is about power; it is about who determines 'the norms by which we live, and by which we define and govern ourselves.' Who decides what is right and wrong…Whose beliefs shall form the basis of law?" Buchanan argued that "our beliefs" grounded in "the Old and New Testament" and "natural law and tradition" were at war with a "destructive, degenerate, ugly, pornographic, Marxist, anti-American ideology." The battle is over "family, faith, friends, and country. For the ashes of their fathers and the temples of their Gods." And the battle was now "raging in our public schools" and the teaching of history. Buchanan claimed, "If a country forgets where it came from, how will its people know who they are?...The battle over our schools is part of the war to separate…all Americans from their heritage."[20]

---

[19] Patrick J. Buchanan, "1992 Republican National Convention Speech," Republican National Convention, Houston, TX (August 17, 1992) <www.buchanan.org>.
[20] Patrick J. Buchanan, "The Cultural War for the Soul of America" (Sept 14, 1992) <www.buchanan.org>.

Perhaps the penultimate book reflecting the most comprehensive articulation of conservative criticisms and concerns over American identity is Samuel P. Huntington's *Who Are We? The Challenges to America's National Identity* (2004).[21] Huntington's fundamental premise on which the whole book rests is America ("We") is "different" and "distinct" from other nations ("thems"),[22] which leads to a tenuous inductive argument: American cultural difference is notably superior because it has produced the most powerful nation on the planet, and that difference is due to a "distinct" Anglo-Protestant culture and its "religiosity." This inductive argument is repeated in numerous forms throughout the book, but it is never proved through scholarly argument and substantial evidence; it is rather assumed to be true via faulty claims, historical inaccuracies, and topically referenced, highly selective, and

[21] Samuel P. Huntington, *Who Are We? The Challenges to America's National Identity* (New York: Simon & Schuster, 2004).
[22] Huntington's discussion of identity is very confused because he tries to meld essentialist Cartesian dualism with modern constructivism, and then hold it together with a fascist militarism. Huntington tells his readers that identities and cultures are "constructed" by people, adapted to environments, and change as environments and peoples change. However, he also posits an unproblematical "substance" or "qualities" of "self" that are "possessed" by a person and which make that individual "distinct." But he further muddies his discussion by saying that identities are not substantial, but contextual, i.e. "to define themselves, people need an other." This contextual discussion argues against a "substantial" core of human identity and instead posits identity as an I/we contextually defined against a you/them, which according to Huntington inevitably leads to "competition," "antagonism," "demonization," and finally the transformation of the "other" into an "enemy" that must be fought and killed (21-26). Without invoking the concept, Huntington is replicating Sartre's critical master/slave dialectic by which Sartre pointed out how human identity and society are replicated through ego-centrism, intolerance, antagonism, violence, and war. Throughout the book Huntington celebrates war as the primary source for national cohesion, unity, and identity, and he devotes a section on "The Search for An Enemy." In this section Huntington claims that that "peace" and the absence of an "enemy" produces "internal disunity," and thus, in order to protect national identity America needed to find an enemy after the Cold War, which turned out to be "militant Islam," "America's first enemy of the twenty-first century" (258-64). Throughout the book Huntington reminds his readers with nationalist glee that it was only after 9-11 and America's militaristic response that a heightened sense of patriotism and nationalism produced a sense of national unity not seen since World War II or the early Cold War (3-4, 199, 264).

superficially engaged reviews the scholarly and polemical literature.[23] Huntington core claim is that America's Anglo-Protestant culture is *alone* responsible for *all* things *distinctly* American: the English language, Christianity, religious commitment, republican concepts (the rule of law, the responsibility of rulers, the rights of individuals, individualism, and the work ethic), and the American creed of equality and freedom. Thus, the Anglo-Protestant culture must be preserved against the rising tides of multiculturalism ("ethnic separatism" and "reverse racism") and Hispanic immigration ("Hispanization") or American will dissipate and "transform" into "a country of two languages, two cultures, and two peoples." And even though the Anglo-Protestant culture has traditionally been a homogeneous, "overwhelmingly white," and white supremacist culture (a fact that Huntington does admit in subdued tones in several places), Huntington argues that "the importance of Anglo-Protestant culture" as *the* foundational cultural identity of Americans does not mean that America is only open to "Anglo-Protestant people." But he is quite clear that ethnic minorities must become Americans on Anglo-Protestant terms (Americanization) or else they are a corrosive threat to a unified national identity: "There is no Americano dream. There is only the American dream created by an Anglo-Protestant society. Mexican-

---

[23] I will provide two examples of Huntington's numerous flawed argumentation and historical inaccuracies. First, Hunting claims that slavery "and its legacies" have been "*the* American dilemma" [author's emphasis], which is demonstrably false. He then sets up a dichotomy. One the one hand laudable and self-less nationalist black leaders like Martin Luther King Jr. sought "equal rights for all" in order to solve this central dilemma. On the other hand there were negative black leaders like Bayard Rustin who helped institute "affirmative discrimination"/"reverse discrimination" through narrow-minded and self-interested demands for "material benefits to blacks as a distinct racial group" (146-158). Huntington admits that the American creed of equal rights for all was "ignored and flouted in practice" for "over two hundred years." The Civil Rights legislation made thing truly equal for the first time in American history and yet he has the audacity to argue that it was black people and affirmative action policies that "reintroduced racial discrimination into American practice" (157). He basically makes the argument that racism disappeared overnight in 1965 only to be reintroduced by greedy blacks who only wanted to profit off the displacement of innocent white Americans. The second flawed argument is representative of his treatment of much of the scholarly literature in this book. Huntington cites Milton Gordon's seminal yet outdated (1964) sociological study of assimilation in America. Instead of a close read of Gordon's central arguments, Huntington just lists off several quotes and makes the claim that while assimilation has "never been complete," it has worked extremely well and is "a great, possibly the greatest, American success story" (183). Huntington's claim completely misrepresents Gordon's argument, which was all successful assimilation in America has been superficial "cultural assimilation" (by which immigrants and minorities adopt the culture and language of the dominant culture), but Gordon went on to demonstrate that many ethnic minorities, especially dark skinned racial minorities, still suffer prejudice and discrimination, and were kept from the more significant "structural assimilation." Huntington makes the demonstrably false claim that all immigrants between 1820 and 1924 were "almost totally assimilated into American society" on equal and welcoming terms (178), and he uses his unfounded assertion to severely criticize newer immigrants as threats to American society, like Mexicans, because there are not assimilating as completely as older generations of immigrants.

Americans will share in that dream and in that society only if they *dream in English*" [my emphasis].[24]

Huntington explained quite clearly in his Foreword that he was motivated by his "own identities as a patriot and a scholar" (it is very significant which identity he named first), and he acknowledged that "the motives of patriotism and of scholarship" could very easily "conflict" with each other. He claims that his scholarship is "detached and thorough" and that it is based upon "an analysis of the evidence," and yet he does admit, "My selection and presentation of that evidence may well be influenced by my patriotic desire to find meaning and virtue in America's past and in its possible future." Throughout the book Huntington engages in the rhetorical fallacy of reifying a nationally unified, distinct, and unambiguously clear "We," which is the voice of the "majority," the American "public." Throughout the book Huntington unproblematically speaks for *the* American people ("We Americans") and claims *the* America "most Americans love and want" is the exact same as *the* America "I know and love," which in turn is the exact opposite of the divisive "cults of multiculturalism" with their Anti-American ("left-wing, socialist, working-class") vision.[25] But Huntington reveals evidence that his position may not be representative of *all* Americans.

In fact, the views and arguments put forth in Huntington's book (and the views and arguments of *all* of the conservative critics surveyed in this essay) resemble very closely Huntington's characterization of "white nativism." One could make a strong argument that Huntington and the other conservative critics are in fact a type of white nativist, which is arguably a small, but powerful and highly vocal minority in America. It is instructive to quote Huntington at length and then compare his words in relation to his central arguments discussed above:

---

[24] Ibid., 365, 9, xv-xvii, 256.
[25] Ibid., xvii, 10-11, 171-73, 144. Huntington engages in classical populist/progressive rhetoric throughout the book by breaking the culture was into a dichotomous debate between the interests of *the* "America people" and the special "minority" interests represented by the "elites." Throughout the book this debate is rhetorically described in terms of a zero-sum competition, whereby, what is good for minorities (multiculturalism) must be detrimental and detracting from *the* American people (nationalism). His rhetorical characterization of multiculturalism-as-minority-rights runs from simplistic-and-unfair ("the idea that diversity rather than unity or community should be America's overriding value") to unfair half-truths ("reverse discrimination") to out right distortions and lies (multiculturalism comes only "at the expense of teaching the values and culture that Americans have had in common") (142, 154, 173).

One very plausible reaction [to multiculturalism fomented in the 1960s] would be the emergence of exclusivist sociopolitical movements composed largely but not only of white males, primarily working-class and middle-class, protesting and attempting to stop or reverse these changes and what they believe, accurately or not, to be the diminution of their social and economic status, their loss of jobs to immigrants and foreign countries, the perversion of their culture, the displacement of their language, and the erosion or even evaporation of the historical identity of their country…the preservation or restoration of what they see as "white America" is a central goal…to defend one's "native" culture and identity and to maintain their purity against foreign influences.

Huntington and the other cultural critics surveyed here seem to represent the "new white nationalists" who are "cultured, intelligent, and often possessing impressive degrees" and who fear that Hispanics and other ethnic and racial minority groups are a "threat to their language, culture, and power." Huntington made it very clear that culture is a human invention and that cultures change, thus, based on his reasoning, Anglo-Protestant America must be preserved not because of some transcendent value, but because it is *his* culture and *he* loves it and he will fight "others," like Hispanics, to keep *his* culture pure and powerful. It is not a noble sentiment, but it is certainly heartfelt.[26]

---

[26] Ibid., xvii, 10-11, 171-73, 144, 309-16.

Liberal Defense of 20th Century Reform

By the mid 1990s left leaning academics began to more fully address the arguments and historiography of conservative critics. Liberal responses were drafted for a number of reasons. Most spent time analyzing conservative falsehoods and exaggerations. Many acknowledged and legitimated several conservative fears, albeit in less extreme and apocalyptic terms. Most put forth counter arguments to justify the essential cultural changes initiated in the 1960s, however, many incorporated conservative critiques in order to reframe and defuse the cultural war in terms of a liberal or multicultural nationalism. There have also been many voices from the political left who pushed for more radical changes. Radicals have often sought to extend the debate of the culture war beyond a narrow preoccupation with American identity, and have focused instead on larger issues of American imperialism, universal human rights, and ecological sustainability. Some radical voices have even suggested that the bounded community of the nation is itself an impediment to social justice as it is based on an exclusivity that can be used to deny human dignity and justice to those like "illegal" immigrants who lie beyond the protection of the nation.

Michael Walzer wrote an important essay, "Pluralism: A Political Perspective" (1980), in which he argued that "national and ethnic pluralism has been the rule, not the exception" in American history. Revolutionary leaders (and many political ideologues and activists since) tried to argue that democracy was only possible if it was accompanied by "cultural unity;" however, as Walzer pointed out, history has shown that democracy and claims for political and social equality have "proven to be the great solvents" of cultural unity rather than its champions. The cultural unification of many peoples under a single nation-state, Walzer argued, "is possible only under tyrannical regimes...except in the United States." The United States is exception in human history because it has been built on the foundation of a "multiracial society," albeit one where most "minority races were politically impotent and socially invisible" for a great part of its history. But Walzer argued that the "repression" of these minority groups did not negatively effect the system of American pluralism constructed through immigration (although he did admit that "racism is the great barrier to a fully developed pluralism"). America has been an "immigrant society" bound by patriotism to political ideals, according to Walzer, not a nation defined by ethnicity or territory. The rise of political pluralism in the 20th century was a reaction to the coercive power of the expanded modern state, which often demanded cultural Americanization on top of political patriotism from immigrants. Pluralists like Horace Kallen defended and celebrated diversity, and argued that America was a "nation of nationalities" and, therefore, in no need of hegemonic unity. This inspired the "ethnic self-assertion" of cultural and racial groups in America during the 20th century, which Walzer claimed were the "functional equivalent of national liberation in other parts of the world." But cultural diversity does not threaten American political identity, argued Walzer, because civil society and the state "though they constantly interact, are formally distinct." Thus, while individuals find solace in cultural group identity in civil society, those same individuals identify with the state of America in politics: "Politics forces [ethnic groups] into alliances and coalitions, and democratic politics, because it recognizes each citizen as the equal of every other, without regard to ethnicity, fosters a unity of individuals alongside the diversity of groups." Besides, the power of the individualism produced by American nationalism has a destabilizing effect on group identity, argued Walzer, and thus pluralism is an "experiment" that "will prove to be a temporary phenomenon, a way-station on the road to American nationalism."[27]

Walzer also wrote another influential essay in 1990, "What Does It Mean to Be an 'American?'" In this essay he claims that "anybody can live [in America], and just about everybody does." American identity is not based on an ethnic or territorial nationalism, but on the "virtue" of immigrants and natives coming together into a single yet diverse people: "the manyness of America is cultural, its oneness is political." America is composed of many ethnic groups but American is not itself an ethnic group. Immigrants retain their former identity but add onto it a hyphenated American identity, which is a political affiliation to a political nation. The hyphen is a "plus sign," not a disavowal of ethnicity. Americans can live "on either side of the hyphen" and still be Americans. National unity comes from citizenship in the nation and "pledging allegiance to the 'one and indivisible' republic," not from cultural conformity. Walzer argued that American nationalism is uniquely "complex" because it is based on the ideas of tolerance and inclusion, "incorporating oneness and manyness in a 'new order.'" This creates for a sort of national "incoherence," but Walzer argues that is part of the distinctive American nation, which is still "radically unfinished" in its nature." Americans are free to "choose" their own cultural location on either side of the hyphen and this freedom keeps America vibrant an

---

[27] Michael Walzer, "Pluralism: A Political Perspective," in *Harvard Encyclopedia of American Ethnic Groups* (Cambridge: Belknap Press of Harvard University, 1980). Reprinted in Michael Walzer, *What It Means to Be an American: Essays on the American Experience* (New York: Marsilio, 1996).

unfettered from a "singular national destiny."[28]

Liah Greenfeld took a few pages at the end of her historical study, *Nationalism: Five Roads to Modernity* (1992), to say a few words about American nationalism for her contemporary context.[29] Greenfeld argued that American nationalism was based on civic nationalist principles of freedom, democracy, and equality enshrined in *The Declaration of Independence*. Not everyone agreed with these principles and these principles were not always practiced, but these were the ideals that defined a nation. The "people" of America were not defined by any ethnic unity because "America has been a nation of immigrants from the beginning." Instead, American nationalism was defined by an association of individuals who gave allegiance to a set of principles and, thus, "pluralism was built into the system" because culture and ethnicity mattered less than the affirmation of nationalist principles. The combination of a pluralist people and a civic nationalism has tended to create a tumultuous yet somehow united republic: Our "national commitment" to the ideals of freedom, equality, and democracy "remains the main source of social cohesion and the main stimulant of unrest in it." Greenfeld argued, "To be an American means to persevere in one's loyalty to the ideals, in spite of the inescapable contradictions between them and reality, and to accept reality without reconciling oneself to it."

Jennifer L. Hochschild defined and contextually explored the American Dream, the most pervasive and powerful nationalist ideology in the U.S.[30] Like all ideologies the American Dream resists a formulaic definition or prescriptive power in terms of predicting the behaviors of Americans who subscribe to its ideological tenets; however, Hochschild attempted to get past the vagueness of the general idea of working hard for material success in order to tease out a more analytical conception of the American Dream. She broke the ideology into four tenets corresponding to four descriptions questions: (1) Who may pursue success? – Everyone can pursue success; (2) What does one pursue? – One pursues "success;" (3) How does one pursue success? – Success is the result of an individual's hard work and self sacrifice; (4) Why is success worth pursing? – Success is a virtue, which both constitutes and demonstrates an individual's worthiness. The pursuit of success is complicated by the ambiguity of "success," which can be defined in absolute, relative, and competitive terms. An absolute definition rests the basic achievement of an individual; a relative definition depends upon the

---

[28] Michael Walzer, "What Does it Mean to Be an 'American?'" *Social Research* (1990); Reprinted in Michael Walzer, *What It Means to Be an American: Essays on the American Experience* (New York: Marsilio, 1996).

[29] Liah Greenfeld, *Nationalism: Five Roads to Modernity* (Cambridge: Harvard University Press, 1992): 482-84.

[30] Jennifer L. Hochschild, *Facing Up to the American Dream: Race, Class, and the Soul of the Nation* (1995; reprint, Princeton: Princeton University Press, 1996).

contextual evaluation of success relative to an external marker like another person's level of success; and a competitive definition corresponds to a capitalist marketplace where only the best will win success. The American dream promotes a "radical individualism" which completely overlooks social and structural mediators like "economic processes, environmental constraints, or political structures." This factor is especially dangerous because American capitalist society is structurally set up to "ensure that some fail, at least relatively, and the dream does nothing to help Americans cope with or even recognize that fact." Hochschild especially looks at the structure of racism in American society and she demonstrated how it has constrained and *continues to constrain* African American success in relation to white Americans and white European immigrants. Many African Americans remain deeply entrenched in poverty and well beyond reach of achieving any measure of the American Dream, and this has caused many African Americans, especially middle-class blacks, to reject the American Dream in order to promote separatist black nationalisms or self-defeating nihilisms. Hochschild argued that the ideology of the American dream is "flawed at the core" because it obscures the structural factors like racism and class that create and sustain inequality. Thus the ideology "under the cloak of individual agency" both gives people "unjustified hopes" and also ensures "unwarranted feelings of failure." The American dream has the capacity to both "deceive" and "liberate" by encouraging "everyone to win" while structurally setting up many to loose. Despite the "inherent flaws" of the ideology of the American dream and Hochschild's "ambivalence" toward the concept, she argued: "For better or for worse, it is *our* ideology, and we are stuck with it. We had better make the best of our situation, and strive to use the strictures of the American dream to enable more Americans to achieve the fantasies lurking within it." However if American society is not structurally transformed, Hochschild delivered a serious warning: "If it can be construed as an *ideal*, a broad, generous, inclusive vision that encourages people to be the best they can be however they define that best, then transformative pluralism and open channels of mobility are direct and plausible extensions of Americans' core tradition. But if it is only an *ideology* in the narrow sense, a self-righteous club that winners use to justify their own actions and to push away, blame, or brainwash losers, then white separatism will continue to flourish, black separatism to grow, and class barriers to harden."[31]

An important liberal response was made in 1995 by Todd Gitlin, a founding member of SDS in the 1960s who had become a sociologist at

---

[31] Ibid., xiv, 15-58, 249, 252, 259.

the University of California, Berkeley.[32] Gitlin framed his discussion of recent culture wars by arguing that certain Americans "who have imagined themselves to be *real* Americans, *normal* Americans" have repeatedly over the course of U.S. history engaged in "purification crusades" to address and combat those groups or individuals who "threaten the integrity of the nation" [his emphasis]. Gitlin argued that the periodic culture wars in American history have tended to obscure contested realities rather than clarify or settle them. Thus, Gitlin argued that all positions and controversies needed to be re-examined in order to not only understand American identity, but also (from his leftist vantage point) to understand "the contemporary incapacity of American politics," by which he meant the failure of the American Left to effectively redirect attention away from symbolic battles and onto more important and pressing social and economic issues.

Gitlin discussed at length many cultural controversies over the politics of identity. Gitlin argued that all sides focused exclusively on symbolic representations instead of concrete social and economic realities: Conservatives, liberals, and minority groups spoke from positions of "moral conviction" and argued over competing "emotional meanings" attached to historical symbols instead of focusing on "rock-bottom class inequalities and racial discrimination." Gitlin argued that the culture wars boiled down to verbal battles over "real and imagined symbols of insult," which did nothing to address the concrete realities of power, racial discrimination, and economic injustice. Both sides simply battled over symbols. Both sides won and lost "symbolic victories." All the while racial discrimination remained, economic injustice increased, and the American public became more divided. Gitlin was especially hard on liberals and the "so-called Left" who had seemingly renounced its older mission of changing material inequalities (especially the oppression of certain classes and races). Gitlin argued that the divisive symbolic battles over "identity politics," the primary arena of the culture wars, marked the "decline" of the American Left. The Left once had a historical mission based on the "universal values" of freedom, justice, equality and the "common good," but after the 1970s it had been fractured and demoralized by "sectarianism," "petty" debates over rhetoric and representation, and the impotence of "false solutions proclaimed for real problems."[33]

While America has always been divided by classes and races, Gitlin argued, there was still a shared moral vision based on the sacred "ideas" consecrated in *The Declaration of Independence*, which framed the debated contours of the nation. For most of American history the

---

[32] Todd Gitlin, *The Twilight of Common Dreams: Why America is Wracked by Culture Wars* (New York: Metropolitan Books, 1995): 2-3.
[33] Ibid., 20, 23, 29-36.

debate between radicals and conservatives was over inclusiveness, not nationality. Conservatives made many attempts to "compress differences" into a "single," normative American WASP identity, which invariably was complicated not only by internal "contradictions," but also by "those *other* Americans" (immigrants, aliens, slaves, radicals, and sects) who had been marginalized, ignored, or eliminated in order to manufacture a *selective* national unity. These "other Americans," the "despised outsiders," constructed their own "unmelted," "torn," and sectarian American identities in opposition to exclusive crusades for a "common culture," but invariably these outsiders sought for political inclusion within the nation. Gitlin pointed out a long tradition of "democratic Americanism." This was a leftist/liberal version of American nationalism, which used the universal moral vision of *The Declaration* to help extend political rights and equality to these outsiders.[34]

However, this democratic Americanism, as Gitlin argued, began to unravel in the 1960s because protest movements and the New Left began to reject both "conventional versions of American identity" and American ideals. This resulted in a reactionary "anti-Americanism" which celebrated diversity, anti-establishmentarianism, and individualism as new ideals. The New Left relinquished all claim to "the idea of a common America" and, thereby, Americanism "was ceded, by default, to the Right." Republicans were able to use revised notions of a common culture and Americanism in order to marshal organized political reaction to the rights revolution of the 1960s. The American Left was fractured into a "collection of interest groups" with no "vocabulary for the common good," and the Democratic party could offer no compelling counter-nationalist vision: "no commonality, no alternative crucible, no compelling rhetoric, no political culture – only a heap of demands piled on demands." Thus, after securing a solid political block based on a nationalist agenda, gaining more and more political power, and eventually claiming victory in the Cold War, the Republican party and social conservatives initiated an all out attack on the liberal welfare-state and declared a wider "war for the soul of America." The Left was fragmented into "partisans of identity politics" and, as Gitlin argued, it could not effectively respond to the powerful conservative reaction. The culture wars were not only initiated by the conservative right, but fought over territory (national identity) that only the right could effectively defend. Thus Gitlin's book is an extended critique of the Left by a Leftist in order to marshal a new universal Leftist vision with which to protect and justify the liberal welfare state and the rights revolution against the

---

[34] Ibid., 45, 48-51, 56-59.

onslaughts of conservative cultural warriors. Gitlin argued that the Left needs to find a way "to cultivate the spirit of solidarity across the lines of difference" in order to "build bridges" and find a common, democratic moral vision. Otherwise, Gitlin warned, the American Left will cease to exist as a political force of any consequence and the conservative counter-revolution will know no bounds.[35]

Michael Lind published a widely read "manifesto" of liberal nationalism called *The Next American Nation* (1995).[36] Lind's central argument: America was and continues to be a "real nation" – "a concrete historical community, defined primarily by a common language, common folkways, and a common vernacular culture." He argued that most Americans identify more with a national identity than they do with any political affiliation, but American nationalism has been poorly defined outside the older chauvinistic boundaries of a "white Christian nation," which was the foundational ethos of the first two "Republics" of America. Lind conceptualized American history as three distinct "Republican" regimes, each defined by specific nationalist ethos and specific nationalist policies. The "First Republic" of "Anglo-America" (1584 to 1850) built upon the strong ethnocultural Anglo-Saxon national community in place before the revolution and it used Protestant Christianity and federal-republicanism to create a national community – the United States of America. The "Second Republic" of Euro-Christian America (1850 to 1960), infused by a nationalist religion of democracy, capitalism, and a Pan-Christian ethic, expanded the national community to include most white Europeans (and after World War II, both Catholics and Jews were accepted); however, the expanded second republic was built on the foundation of a white supremacist Herrenvolk (master-race) caste-system, which actively excluded and subjected non-white races. The "Third Republic" of multicultural America (1960s to current) was a minority led reaction to the white supremacy of the first two Republics. Multicultural America began as a Civil Rights Revolution, which sought to open up the American nation by securing formal legal and political rights for all American citizens; however, in an effort to further extend equality-as-opportunity to equality-as-result, a federal system of racial categorization and an institutionalized "racial preference system" was put into place (affirmative action) to "force racial quotas" on American society. What Lind called "The Second Radical Reconstruction" was a federally enforced system of minority preference, which meant to

---

[35] Ibid., 68-73, 79, 82, 100-01, 146, 165, 198-99, 207, 217, 236-37.
[36] Michael Lind, *The Next American Nation: The New Nationalism and the Fourth American Revolution* (New York: Free Press, 1995). Lind claimed that his book was "the first manifesto of American liberal nationalism" (15).

"remedy" racial, class, and gender discrimination in social spheres like schooling and employment. While Lind was sympathetic to the rationale of affirmative action, he criticized it as an intrusive, unfair, divisive, and dangerous policy.[37]

Lind specifically took issue with multicultural America's obsession with race and culture as *the* foundational source of identity: He claimed it was not in the best interests of the American people. Lind argued that discussion of culture was often a veiled reduction of race, and thus, cultural authenticity and cultural pride were often calls to adhere to a certain biologically defined and essentialist identity. He called the priorities of multiculturalism divisive because "identity politics" were eclipsing identification with a larger national community and with larger national issues (like economics and health care). Like Gitlin, Lind also called multicultural identity politics a dangerous distraction from identifying the real and continued source of inequality in America: the "white power structure." Lind argued that the white power structure used multiculturalism and racial preferences fraudulently to "provide the illusion of integration, while imposing minimal costs on the white overclass:" it was a classic imperial case of divide and rule.[38] This explains why during the supposedly more equal and fair regime of multicultural America, there was a silent "revolution of the rich," whereby, income inequality increased dramatically. Lind argued that multiculturalism socially and politically fragmented the majority of Americans by allowing "culture wars" to displace "class wars," and thus, unified elites were able to initiate and win "a generation-long class war," which has led to a "new Feudalism." Lind argued that multiculturalism was destroying the national integrity of America, it was fragmenting the American people, and it was solidifying the power structure of a white overclass.[39]

To renew and rebuild America, Lind argued for a revised liberal nationalism, which would be the foundational ethos for a new "fourth republic" of the United States of America. Liberal nationalism would build on the notion that America is an ethnocultural nation unified by a common language, folkways, memories, and mores, but it would also be an inclusive "mixed-race culture" symbolically defined as a "transracial melting pot," which Lind called "Trans-America." Lind argued that the U.S. should be a "multiracial and multireligious but unicultural American

---

[37] Ibid., 5-9, 20-27, 55, 65-70, 89, 97-115, 119.
[38] Lind argued, "Racial preference is in reality a conservative policy, a form of elaborate but ultimately superficial tokenism that is much less costly, to affluent whites in general and the business class in particular, than expensive universal programs designed to improve the educations and standard of living of the bottom half of the population, of all races. Compared to color-blind liberalism, racial preference is cheap" (179).
[39] Ibid., 123, 130-31, 139, 141, 181-85, 188-215, 245.

ethnic nation." He held up blacks as the quintessential Americans because they not only left behind their older cultures, but mixed and blended into the emerging American identity, which prefigured their actual inclusion into the political state as citizens. Lind argued that nationalism has often been the tool of the political left in efforts to promote "greater political, social, and economic equality among all members of the national community." In an effort to bring Americans together, Lind argued that a shared set of ancestors is unimportant. The important factor for a renewed America is sharing a contemporary cultural and political union – a national community – in order to produce shared common descendants: Americans.[40]

David A. Hollinger wrote a widely influential work called *Postethnic America: Beyond Multiculturalism* (1995).[41] Hollinger argued that the ideology and socio-political movement of multiculturalism has served a useful purpose in attacking a racist Anglo-Protestant based American culture; however, he argued that the blunt race/culture ("ethno-racial") based framework of multiculturalism is limited in understanding and dealing with "the problem of boundaries" in what is *becoming* a "postethnic," "cosmopolitan," and trans/multinational world, which is developing more acute globalized problems that need global solutions. The traditional conceptions of ethnicity have posited assumed, often monolithic, and sometimes racialized "identities," which mask the degree of actual "affiliation" any given individual psychologically and socially invests in a particular ethnic group to which that individual is supposed to belong. Hollinger uses the example of Alex Haley and conceptualized "Haley's choice," by which he theorized the choice Haley made in tracing his "roots" back to his black mother's ancestors in Africa rather than identifying with his white father's ancestors in Ireland. Now while Hollinger did admit that a racialized and racist America circumscribed and forced Haley's choice, Hollinger went on to argue that in a less segregated and increasing mixed ethno-racial world, individuals are becoming freer to choose ethnic, mixed ethnic, or non-ethnic identities, but the ethno-racially infused multicultural ethos is unprepared to handle these new volitional and mixed identity formations. Hollinger's conception of a hybrid, postethnic America recognizes the complexity of identity, whereby, individuals constantly shift between many situationally defined and sometimes conflicting identities. Hollinger argued that America should shed its "*ethnic* history" and embrace its "*non*ethnic ideology of the nation" as a means to embrace and foster a "*post*ethnic future." Hollinger asked his readers to take seriously the national motto

---

[40] Ibid., 259-98.
[41] David A. Hollinger, *Postethnic America: Beyond Multiculturalism* (1995; reprinted & expanded, New York: Basic Books, 2005).

E Pluribus Unum as a way to conceptualize cultural diversity united by a national commitment to a common creed of liberty and justice. "Individuals should be allowed to affiliate or disaffiliate with their won communities of descent to an extent that they choose," argued Hollinger, "while affiliating with whatever nondescent communities are available and appealing to them." What unites these highly diverse and hybrid individuals is a democratically organized state "defined by a civic principle of nationality" and enacted in a shared "national culture" where diverse individuals democratically deliberate and work towards a "common future:" "The national community's fate can be common without its will being uniform, and the nation can constitute a common project without effacing all of the various projects that its citizens pursue through their voluntary affiliations."[42]

Gary Gerstle's "Liberty, Coercion, and the Making of Americans" (1997) looked at the Crevecoeurian myth of Americanization and how it affected the historical and sociological study of cultural assimilation and Americanization.[43] Gerstle argued that Crevecoeur's conception of assimilation in *Letters from an American Farmer* was one of the "most influential mediations on what it means to become an American." Not only did the Crevecoeurian myth help define the early 20th century ideal of the "melting pot," but it also influenced the way 20th century sociologists and historians conceptualized theories of assimilation, which in tern had an influence on public policy and debate. Invoking radical scholars of the 1960s and the new scholarship of David R. Roediger and others, Gerstle criticized neo-Crevecoeurian scholars for not focusing enough on the complexity and constraints (class, gender, race, nation) of the Americanization process by which "social forces external to the immigrant" play a very significant, if not the most significant, role in the Americanization of immigrants. Gerstle argued that these "structure of power" limited the options of immigrants (and also often coerced) during the assimilation/Americanization process. Gerstle criticized the overly optimistic accounts make by Fuchs, Sollors and Hollinger who seemed to argue for a theory of personal agency and a fluidness to identity that did not take into account the restrictiveness of structural constraints (especially race, as Gerstle argued, "race, even more than class and gender, still limits the options of those who seek to become American"). Gerstle clearly believed that "historical circumstances and social structures undermined experiments in the fashioning of identity."

---

[42] Ibid., 1, 6-7, 19-28, 82-84, 106, 116, 132-34, 143, 157.
[43] Gary Gerstle, "Liberty, Coercion, and the Making of Americans," *The Journal of American History* 84:2 (Sept 1997): 524-58.

Gerstle looked to newer studies on gender and working class Americanism (including his own), which have created a "synthesis between agency and structure" and, thereby, demonstrated how "Americanization involves both inventiveness and constraint:" America was not "simply a Crevecoeurian land of possibility," it was also "a land of constraint."

> becoming American cannot be understood in "emancipationist" terms alone, for immigrants invariably encountered structures of class, race, gender, and national power that constrained, and sometimes defeated, their efforts to be free. Coercion, as much as liberty, has been intrinsic to our history and to the process of becoming American.

Gerstle also critiqued liberal American nationalism via David Hollinger's *Postethnic America*. Gerstle agreed with Hollinger that liberal nationalism infused and largely defined Progressivism, the New Deal, the civil rights movement, and the Great Society by "derviv[ing] legitimacy from their claim to speak 'on behalf of the American nation' as a whole." However, Gerstle also argued that nationalism by definition means "boundaries" and "internal and external opponents," and thus the "equality" gained over 1930 to 1960 was "made possible by the coercion of the 1910s and 1920s:"

> America had shrunk its circle of the 'we' and had substantially narrowed the range of acceptable cultural and political behavior...The success of this liberal nationalist project, I would argue, depended on the earlier deployment of the coercive power of the state against Germans, new immigrants, Asians, and political radicals. Liberal progress, in this instance, profited from the earlier period of repression and exclusion...Historians have yet to take full measure of the powerful nationalism that settled over American in the 1910s and 1920s, suffocating the hyphenated identities...weken[ing] the pluralist character of pre-1917 America and accelerat[ing] national integration.

Gerstle is but one example of many leftist critiques of liberal nationalism. Historians have begun to examine the artificial boundaries of the nation, what Robert Wiebe called "fictive kin composites," and they have started to historically contextualize nations in relation to other nations and in relation to non-national and transnational paradigms of a global age.[44] Bonnie Honig has looked into multiple versions of immigrants myths in relation to nationalism, and she argued that

---

[44] Thomas Bender, ed., *Rethinking American History in a Global Age* (Berkeley: University of California Press, 2002).

nationalist discourses that focus on immigrants do so in order to "renationalize" the state by justifying the inclusiveness of a bounded and exclusivist national community that still derives its identity by "pitting 'us' against 'them.'" She argued instead for a "democratic cosmopolitanism" by which "citizenship is not just a druidical status distributed (or not) by states, but a *practice* in which denizens, migrants, residents, and the allies hold states accountable for their definitions and distributions of goods, powers, rights, freedoms, privileges, and justice...denationalize the state in order to make room for the generation of alternative sites of affect and identity against which states often guard."[45] John Exdell has criticized liberal nationalism for "legitimiz[ing] a policy of exclusion," which leaves open the possibility of further nationalist exclusions based on ethnicity and race. Liberals claim that solidarity and justice within the bounded community are produced and protected by nationalist identity; however, Exdell demonstrated that national solidarity in America has been and continues to be undermined by the divisive power of race via a long tradition of white supremacist American ethnonationalism. Exdell questions the liberal assumption that a reformation of "national self-understanding" is enough to truly "unite" American citizens and overcome a long tradition of American racism. Exdell instead asked if new infusions of Latino immigrants might "renew" and "revitalize" American identity by developing a "new post-national identity" that might redefine American citizenship as a situated democratic performance conducted by *any* free, productive, and contributing agent within the national territory.[46]

---

[45] Bonnie Honig, *Democracy and the Foreigner* (Princeton: Princeton University Press, 2001): 74-75, 104-5, 122.

[46] John Exdell, "Liberal Nationalism, Immigration, and Race," at *Reclaiming Democracy: Visions and Practices from the Radical Left,* Radical Philosophy Association, 7th Biennial Conference, Creighton University, Omaha, Nebraska, November 4, 2006.

Culture Wars in Context:
Transformations of the American Nation, 1776 to 1990

The modern usage of the terms "nation" and "nationalism" comes from 16th century England. The political discourse of a "nation" became associated with a "people." Reference to a "people" before this time was usually derogatory ("rabble," "plebs," or "mass"), but within the context of 16th century England a "people" became glorified as the source of sovereignty and the sole object of political loyalty. This political definition of a nation stressed a civic conception of individual sovereignty (as opposed to monarchical sovereignty) constituted by a constitutional law (as opposed to divinity or monarchical absolutism). However, national identity was also an ideological and social construction. The notion of a sovereign people was an "imagined community" that gave its members identity, affiliation, community, and purpose. Isaiah Berlin described nationalism as manufacturing a "kind of homogeneity" out of "common ancestry, common language, customs, traditions, memories, continuous occupancy of the same territory" so as to create "solidarity" while marking off "differences" (usually in the form of an "aggressive chauvinism") between political and social groups. As a political and social ideology, nationalism reveres and reifies the "unity" and "self-determination" of the sovereign people. Loyalty and fidelity to the nation qua people, Berlin argued, is assigned a "supreme value." This secular reverence for a distinct people often leads to an exclusive "ethnic" chauvinism, whereby, membership in a "unique," special, or exceptional people is restricted to an inherited and biologically based group. Nationalism can also be used for more aggressively expansionist political purposes. Powerful ethnic groups or nations can engage in hegemony through which they aggressively (though not necessarily imperialistically) drive for an expanded territory or nation under the banner of "unification" for economic, political, and/or military purposes. This type of nationalism can lead to a federation, an empire, and or "irredentism," whereby, territory and peoples are coercively agglomerated under the control of a centralized and often authoritarian state. But rhetorically conceptualizing nations and peoples as a distinct and uniform social entity needs to be qualified. Nations are rarely based on a distinctly singular "people," a single national ideology, a single state, a single language, or a single territory. Nor does the existence of nationalism necessarily predict the ideological affiliations or standardized behavior of the people within a nation. Nations are imagined communities that represent an idealized and normative "people" that can never actually exist.[47]

The political need to establish and legitimate a people – a *nation* – was a relatively novel and very radical political problem in the 18th century. Nationhood was influenced by the rise of Enlightenment republican/democratic political philosophy and capitalism, and forged through the republican revolutions in England (17th century), America, and France (late 18th century).[48] While the study of nationalism is currently a young social-scientific field of study,[49] the evidence seems to suggest that prior to the late 18th century, only one nation-qua-nation existed: the British. Liah Greenfeld explained how an English national consciousness developed in the 16th century through the power politics of aristocracy, which led to a redefinition of nobility as "service to the nation." In the 17th century affiliation with the British nation expanded due to several factors: the rising middle class who exuded a strong sense of political ownership and entitlement, the expansion of literacy through Protestantism, counter-Reformation repression by Catholic monarchs, and

---

[47] Liah Greenfeld, *Nationalism: Five Roads to Modernity* (Cambridge: Harvard University Press, 1992): 4-14; Guido Zernatto, "Nation: The History of a Word," *Review of Politics* 6 (1944): 351-66; Max Weber, *Wirtschaft und Gesellschaft* in *From Max Weber: Essays in Sociology*, H. H. Gerth and C. Wright Mills, eds. (1946; reprint, Oxford: Oxford University Press, 1958), 171-79; Louis Wirth, "Types of Nationalism," *The American Journal of Sociology* 41 (May 1936): 723-37; Hans Kohn, "The Nature of Nationalism," *The American Political Science Review* 33 (Dec 1939): 1001-21; Chong-Do Hah and Jeffrey Martin, "Toward a Synthesis of Conflict and Integration Theories of Nationalism," *World Politics* 27 (April 1975): 361-86; Isaiah Berlin, "Nationalism: Past Neglect and Present Power," *Against the Current: Essays in the History of Ideas*, in *The Proper Study of Mankind: An Anthology of Essays*, Henry Hardy and Roger Hausheer, eds. (1979; reprint, New York: Farrar, Straus and Giroux, 1997): 581-604; Benedict Anderson, *Imagined Communities: Reflections on the Origin and Spread of Nationalism* (1983; reprint, London: Verso, 1991); Eric Hobsbawm, *Nations and Nationalism since 1780: Programme, Myth, Reality* (1990; reprint, Cambridge: Cambridge University Press, 2000).
[48] Eric Hobsbawm, *The Age of Revolution, 1789 – 1848* (1962; reprint, New York: Vintage Books, 1996); Eric Hobsbawm, *The Age of Capital, 1848 – 1875* (1975; reprint, New York: Vintage Books, 1996); Eric Hobsbawm, *The Age of Empire, 1875 – 1914* (1987; reprint, New York: Vintage Books, 1989); Eric Hobsbawm, *Nations and Nationalism since 1780: Programme, Myth, Reality* (1990; reprint, Cambridge: Cambridge University Press, 2000).
[49] Anthony Smith, "Nationalism and Classical Social Theory," *The British Journal of Sociology* 34 (Mar 1983): 19-38; Eric Hobsbawm, *Nations and Nationalism since 1780: Programme, Myth, Reality* (1990; reprint, Cambridge: Cambridge University Press, 2000); Louis Wirth, "Types of Nationalism," *The American Journal of Sociology* 41 (May 1936): 723-37; Hans Kohn, "The Nature of Nationalism," *The American Political Science Review* 33 (Dec 1939): 1001-21; Liah Greenfeld, "The Trouble with Social Science," *Critical Review* 17:1-2 (2005): 101-16.

finally a republican revolution.[50]   American nationalism was in many ways, but not all, derivative of English nationalism because as Greenfeld and others have argued, "The English settlers came with a national identity;" however, the development of a specific American national identity (as with all national identities) was a highly unique and non-transferable process.   American nationalism took almost a century after the Revolution to develop and diffuse because while the colonists had an emerging "American identity," it was not linked with "a sense that Americans constituted a unity" and, thus, the highly diverse and localized colonies were always "in perpetual peril of dissolving:" As Liah Greenfeld argued, "The forces that could (and eventually did) bring the United States to the brink of disintegration were at least as strong as those which fostered unity."[51]

Polemicists from the political left and right have claimed that an American identity has existed from the first settlements in the 16th and 17th centuries;[52] however, most historians and sociologists have traced the origins of a distinctly American national identity to the mid 19th century, especially after the Civil War, although some historians like Robert Wiebe place the formation of a *national* American identity closer to the end of the 19th century.[53]   Before the Revolution, the largely English colonies were divided by diverse ethnic identities, dispersed regional settlements, and highly localized economies connected more with Europe than each other.   American nationalists had to contend with and overcome

---

[50] Liah Greenfeld, *Nationalism: Five Roads to Modernity*, Ibid., 27-87.

[51] Ibid., 400-02, 424, 426, 431, 444.

[52] Robert A. Carlson, *The Quest for Conformity: Americanization through Education* (New York: John Wiley and Sons, 1975); Michael Lind, *The Next American Nation: The New Nationalism and the Fourth American Revolution* (New York: Free Press, 1995); Samuel P. Huntington, *Who Are We? The Challenges to America's National Identity* (New York: Simon & Schuster, 2004).

[53] Alexis de Tocqueville, *Democracy in America*, Harvey C. Mansfield and Delba Winthrop, trans. & eds. (1835, 1840; reprint, Paris: Editions Gallimard, 1992; reprint, Chicago: University of Chicago Press, 2000); Joyce Appleby, Lynn Hunt, and Margaret Jacob, "History Makes a Nation," in *Telling the Truth About History* (New York: W. W. Norton & Company, 1994): 91-125; David M. Potter, "The Historian's Use of Nationalism and Vice Versa," *The American Historical Review* 67 (July 1962): 924-50; Liah Greenfeld, *Nationalism: Five Roads to Modernity* (Cambridge: Harvard University Press, 1992); Robert H. Wiebe, *The Search For Order, 1877 – 1920* (New York: Hill and Wang, 1967); Robert Wiebe, "Framing U.S. History: Democracy, Nationalism, and Socialism," in *Rethinking American History in a Global Age*, Thomas Bender, ed. (Berkeley: University of California Press, 2002): 236-49; William Earl Weeks, "American Nationalism, American Imperialism: An Interpretation of United States Political Economy, 1789-1861," *Journal of the Early Republic* 14 (Winter 1994): 485-95.

what became a highly diverse colonial federation.[54]   A rhetorically imagined national public – "We the people" – was first manufactured by Revolutionary leaders as a means to unify the diverse and fragmented colonies during the Revolutionary War and again during the debates over the Constitution.[55]   Citizenship was a divisive issue from the very start. Noah Pickus argued that most early leaders agreed that civic principles and a "shared sense of nationhood" needed to be at the core of the new country and its founding documents, but many "differed deeply as the meaning of that nation and whether it could change."[56]

Federalists wanted a small and homogeneous republic with narrowly defined rights of citizenship limited to self-governing, propertied, "virtuous" men, while Anti-Federalists and Jeffersonian Republicans wanted a more "broadly defined national identity" based on universal civic principles and open to all who embraced and abided by those principles. Although the early nation was quite diverse and

---

[54] Thomas J. Archdeacon, *Becoming American: An Ethnic History* (New York: The Free Press, 1983); Karen Ordahl Kupperman, "International at the Creation: Early Modern American History," in *Rethinking American History in a Global Age*, Thomas Bender, ed. (Berkeley: University of California Press, 2002): 103–22; Linda K. Kerber, "The Republican Ideology of the Revolutionary Generation," *American Quarterly* 37 (Autumn 1985): 474-495; Daniel T. Rodgers, "Republicanism: The Career of a Concept," *The Journal of American History* 79 (June 1992): 11-38; Joyce Appleby, "Republicanism and Ideology," *American Quarterly* 37 (Autumn 1985): 461-473; Liah Greenfeld, *Nationalism: Five Roads to Modernity* (Cambridge: Harvard University Press, 1992); Robert Shalhope, "Anticipating Americanism: An Individual Perspective on Republicanism in the Early Republic," In *Americanism: New Perspectives on the History of an Ideal*, Michael Kazin and Joseph A. McCartin, eds. (Chapel Hill: The University of North Carolina Press, 2006): 53-72.

[55] As John Jay famously wrote: Americans were one people "descended from the same ancestors, speaking the same language, professing the same religion, attached to the same principles of government, very similar in their manners and customs." However, Michael Walzer has argued that the American constitution embodied the fragmented cultural diversity of the new republic. The constitution is not one, but "two texts" (the Constitution and the Bill of Rights). Walzer argues that the Bill of Rights actually "opposes" the Constitution by securing protection for diversity. Michael Walzer, "Constitutional Rights and the Shape of Civil Society," *What it Means to Be an American: Essays on the American Experience* (New York: Marsilio, 1996): 105-24. Linda K. Kerber, "The Revolutionary Generation: Ideology, Politics, and Culture in the Early Republic," in *The New American History*, Eric Foner, ed., 2ⁿᵈ ed. (Philadelphia: Temple University Press, 1997): 31-59; Joseph J. Ellis, *Founding Brothers: The Revolutionary Generation* (2000; reprint, New York: Vintage Books, 2002); Alexander Hamilton, James Madison, and John Jay, *The Federalist*. Benjamin Fletcher Wright, ed. (1787-1788; reprint, Cambridge: Harvard University Press, 1961; reprint, New York: Metrobooks, 2002): see especially #1, #2, #6, and #10; G. Calloway, *The American Revolution in Indian Country: Crisis and Diversity in Native American Communities* (Cambridge: Cambridge University Press, 1995); Liah Greenfeld, *Nationalism: Five Roads to Modernity* (Cambridge: Harvard University Press, 1992): 422-23.

[56] Noah Pickus, *True Faith and Allegiance: Immigration and American Civic Nationalism* (Princeton: Princeton University Press, 2005).

divisive, Federalists, like John Jay, tried to manufacture consent for a more homogeneous nation and a more circumscribed citizenship by rhetorically invoking a "one united people – a people descended from the same ancestors, speaking the same language, professing the same religion, attached to the same principles of government, very similar in manners and customs."

While the Constitution seemed to sidestep this debate (there is no formal definition of citizenship in the Constitution) The Declaration of Independence implied a "volitional and contractual" approach to citizenship, which the Constitution did not limit in any way (for instance, there were no "cultural, religious, or linguistic tests for citizenship"). George Washington even went so far as to declare America "open to receive not only the opulent and respectable strange, but the oppressed and persecuted of all nations and religions." But he also gave hint to certain limitations by stating, "We shall welcome [them] to a participation of all our rights and privileges, if by decency and propriety of conduct they appear to merit the enjoyment." This ambivalence infused the parameters of the first Naturalization Law of 1790, which limited citizenship to "free white persons" with two years of residency a good character, and sworn allegiance to the Constitution.[57] The central limitation of free "white" persons was borrowed from the colonial laws of many states and was deliberately used to exclude blacks[58] and Native Americans from the American nation, although overall, Pickus notes, the Naturalization Act was "remarkably inclusive for its time, in bestowing citizenship on all European immigrants." Pickus argued that while European immigrants were considered "central" to the "national-building task of Americanizing the Americans," he also acknowledged that "belonging to the nation and reverence for its traditions mattered," which, in combination with the racial classification of citizenship, definitely circumscribed the bounds of citizenship in the U.S. and seemed to lean more towards legitimating the definition of America in terms of the Federalists' homogenous white republic.[59]

---

[57] The Naturalization Act of 1795 extended the residency requirement to five years and added the requirement that the immigrant declare intention to naturalize at least three years in advance. It also required applicants to renounce all family titles and titles of nobility. Citizenship was restricted further through the Sedition Act, Alien Enemies Act, Alien Friends Act, and the Naturalization Act of 1798 whereby residency requirements were extended to 14 years and new powers gave the president wide latitude to arrest and deport aliens (34-51).

[58] Pickus explained that many of the Founding generation believed that slavery was immoral and should be discontinued, but this did not mean that they wanted to extend citizenship rights to freed blacks or welcome them into civil society. Even most abolitionists who believed blacks to be inherently equal to whites did not think that freed black slaves could assimilate into American society. The "free white" clause in the Naturalization Act was meant to forestall any thought of incorporating blacks into civil society should slavery eventually be abolished (56-58, 61-62).

[59] Ibid., 15, 17, 19, 22-23, 24-25, 34-51, 53-62.

For the next one hundred years there was "no single standard for membership" in the U.S. as "modes of citizenship" were "multiple," "often contradictory" due to their regulation and facilitation by state and local governments, and they were "contested in many ways" by individuals and groups. Citizenship opened up considerably in 1868 with the passage of the Fourteenth Amendment, which enshrined the notion of birthright citizenship to help enfranchise blacks. The Expatriation Act of 1868 reinforced the notion that citizenship was the right of Americans by birth and "relinquishing" it depended on the "consent of the individual." However, Congress also passed the Chinese Exclusion Act in 1882, which narrowed the boundaries of U.S. citizenship by denying Chinese (and most Asians in general) from citizenship (although the Supreme Court in 1886 and 1898 did allow Chinese the principle of rights while in American and did affirm that Chinese children born in America were by right Americans). But citizenship was highly dependent upon "local discretion" as some states extended rights like voting to non-citizens, while other states circumscribed and limited the rights of particular groups who were entitled to full citizenship. Pickus argued that "both the civic and the nationalist dimensions of citizenship had inclusionary and exclusionary consequences." The courts used a nationalist framework and affirmed "whiteness" as the core value of American citizenship, but broad definitions of whiteness allowed more and more Europeans to be accepted as potential citizens. The nationalist principle of birthright citizenship also extended the bounds of citizenship. It even had the ability to circumvent the "whiteness" clause. At the same time civic notions of citizenship based on individual virtue and consent were used to limit or exclude blacks and Native Americans from becoming citizens. And many nativists used a white supremacist version of nationalism to call into question the more open nationalist conception of birthright citizenship.[60]

Throughout the 19th century, national identity and citizenship were ideologically contested battlefields wherein different factions vied for legitimacy, justice, and power.[61] Perhaps the most important,

---

[60] Ibid., 64-71.
[61] Michael Kazin & Joseph A. McCartin, "Introduction," In *Americanism: New Perspectives on the History of an Ideal*, Michael Kazin & Joseph A. McCartin, eds. (Chapel Hill: The University of North Carolina Press, 2006): 1-21; Robert James Branham, "'Of These I Sing": Contesting 'America,'" *American Quarterly* 48:4 (1996): 623-52; Linda K. Kerber, "The Revolutionary Generation: Ideology, Politics, and Culture in the Early Republic," in *The New American History*, Eric Foner, ed., 2nd ed. (Philadelphia: Temple University Press, 1997): 31-59; Eric Foner, *The Story of American Freedom* (New York: W. W. Norton & Co., 1998); Reginald Horsman, *Race and Manifest Destiny: The Origins of American Racial Anglo-Saxonism* (Cambridge: Harvard University Press, 1981); Mia Bay, "See Your Declaration Americans!!! Abolitionism, Americanism, and the Revolutionary Tradition in Free Black Politics," In *Americanism: New Perspectives on the History of an Ideal*, Michael

complex, and emotionally charged 19th century debate over American nationalism was the Civil War and the issue of slavery, which boiled beyond words into violent confrontation.[62] The Civil War enlarged the powers of the nation-state via an expanded bureaucracy, an aggressive executive branch, a conscripted and mobilized federal army, and coordinated communication systems. After the war a new sense of American qua Republican identity, nationality, and purpose was consecrated (and federally enforced in the South), and it would be refined and reinforced through Indian wars, increased immigration, and westward expansion. If the American Revolution and the ratification of the Constitution marked the first crisis in American nationalism, then the Civil War marked the second. Arguably the third major crisis of American nationalism emerged at the end of the 19th century. The Populist, labor and Progressive movements initiated in the late 19th century represented a diverse and widespread sense of national emergency, and their congealed efforts aimed at nothing less than a redefinition of American national identity and purpose, which reverberated an ethos of liberal reform throughout the 20th century.

Nell Irvin Painter's award winning treatment of the Progressive Era, *Standing at Armageddon: The United States, 1877 – 1919*,[63] argued that the central political conflict of the late 19th century was a "struggle over the distribution of wealth and power" – a constant struggle in American history. In 1890 the supper rich (0.01% of the population or about 125,000 families) earned an income of about $264,000 and owned over 50.8% of the national wealth. The upper-middle class (11% of the population and about 1.3 million families) made on average about $16,000 per year and owned about 35% of the national wealth. The remaining 88% of the population (11 million families) earned under $1,500 a year and owned just over 14% of the national wealth, and half of these families (44% of the population) were impoverished, earning less than $150 a year (the poverty level is estimated at around $544 a year for a family). Painter stressed that while income does provide the "single clearest indicator of class standing," the notion of class needs to be seen

---

Kazin and Joseph A. McCartin, eds. (Chapel Hill: The University of North Carolina Press, 2006): 25-52.

[62] David M. Potter, "The Historian's Use of Nationalism and Vice Versa," *The American Historical Review* 67 (July 1962): 924-50; Roger L. Ransom, *Conflict and Compromise: The Political Economy of Slavery, Emancipation, and the American Civil War* (1989; reprint, Cambridge: Cambridge University Press, 1995); Eric Foner, *Forever Free: The Story of Emancipation and Reconstruction* (New York: Alfred A. Knopf, 2005).

[63] Nell Irvin Painter, *Standing at Armageddon: The United States, 1877 – 1919* (New York: W. W. Norton & Company, 1987): xii-xiii, xix, xxiv, xl, xliii, 279-80.

as a complex, "fluid" and ever changing classification. There was no single "middle class," but rather several "middle classes" and also "many ethnicities and races" within each class. The elite classes at the time had the most at stake in the structure of society because they benefited from the distribution of political and economic resources. To protect their interests, the socially and politically powerful and their agents liked to put forth ideological arguments for the "identity of interest." This belief conceptualized society as a smoothly functioning and united organism, wherein, the interests of the great capitalists and property owners were supposedly the best interests of all in society, and further, it was put forth that society operated in harmony with "laws of God or Science."

Reformers of various social and political stripes put forth a counter-conception of society in order to justify what they saw as needed reform. Seeing their own middle-class or working-class interests at odds with those of capitalists and industrialists, democratizers saw society torn by a "conflict of interests." Reformers often, but not always, tried to point out the interests of the "disadvantaged" within the social system and, thereby, argue for "the ideal of equity" and democracy, in order to confront the dangerous extremes of wealth and privilege. But lurking at the periphery of all calls for reform was the specter of working class unrest, which from time to time had boiled into a froth and caused conflicts of interest to turn into real (and often violent) social and political struggles for power. The so called "Progressive Era" was marked by a widespread call for reform and social change, however, as Painter pointed out, "the broadening consensus that change was necessary did not include agreement on the direction or extent of these changes."

In the 1960s another generation of reformers pointed out not only the inequality between the rich and the poor, but also the differential wealth between racial groups, especially between whites and blacks. In the early 1960s the top 20% of Americans possessed 77% of the nation's wealth, while those in the bottom 20% owned only 0.05%. In 1959 22.4% of the population lived in poverty. However, the situation was worse for African Americans. In 1965 43% of all black families earned less than $3,000 a year and were living in poverty (the national rate was 15%). In 1967 39.3% of all black persons in America lived in poverty compared to only 11% of whites. In 1962 the average black income was about 55% of the average income of whites and black unemployment was double the rate of white unemployment. The Civil Rights movement of the 1960s addressed the larger issues of wealth and poverty in America, but the main part of the early movement focused mostly on the legal and social segregation of African Americans and the unjust social and economic treatment they received as second-class citizens. One of the early sparks of the Civil Rights movement was indicative of blacks' oppressed social and political position in U.S. society: in 1955 a young fourteen-year old African American boy named Emmett Till was abducted, bound with barbed wire, mercilessly beaten until his face began to fall off, and thrown into a river to die. His crime was whistling a white woman.[64]

But the Civil Rights movement of the 1960s did not confine itself to just the platforms of economic inequality or the oppression of African Americans. One Civil Rights organization at the time, Students for a Democratic Society, published a widely printed and influential manifesto called *The Port Huron Statement* (1962), which discussed both economic inequality and racial discrimination, but it also outlined issues for reform in both educational and foreign policy as well as larger values along with a political vision of American society. This manifesto even reached beyond American politics and professed support for reform and revolutionary movements around the globe, particularly anti-colonial uprisings in Africa and Asia.[65] The reformist and revolutionary rhetoric of the 1960s inspired many minority groups in America who felt their voices and socio-political issues were being excluded by the mainstream Civil Rights platform. Women played an important role in both the African American Civil Rights programs and in Students for a Democratic Society, however, many women eventually branched off into their own "women's liberation movement" in order to address "the woman question."[66] Mexican Americans drew on a history of organizational efforts in America and several Chicano Civil Rights organizations were formed, including the League of United Latin American Citizens (LULAC), which worked for the "economic, political, and social rights for all Mexican Americans." The Chicano

---

[64] William H. Chafe, *The Unfinished Journey: America Since World War II*, 2nd ed. (1986; revised, Oxford: Oxford University Press, 1991): 146-76, 236-37. Stanley Nelson (director & producer), *The Murder of Emmett Till*, American Experience (produced by WGBH Educational Foundation, distributed by PBS Home Video, 2003). Lawrence Mishel, Jared Bernstein, and Sylvia Allegretto, *The State of Working America 2006/2007*, An Economic Policy Institute Book (Ithaca, NY: ILR Press, an imprint of Cornell University Press, 2007): 283-91. Michael Harrington, *The Other America: Poverty in the United States* (1962; revised, New York: Penguin Books, 1981): 185-202, Ch 4.
[65] Tom Hayden, *The Port Huron Statement: the Visionary Call of the 1960s Revolution* (1962; reprinted, New York: Thunder's Mouth Press, 2005); Todd Gitlin, *The Sixties: Years of Hope, Days of Rage* (New York: Bantam Books, 1987).
[66] Ruth Rosen, *The World Split Open: How the Modern Women's Movement Changed America* (New York: Penguin Books, 2000): Ch 4.

"movimiento" specifically addressed the second-class citizenship of Mexican Americans who were often portrayed as "dehumanized" "commodities" of the American economy.[67] Many other minority social groups in America also became inspired by the large Civil Rights reform movements, including Native Americans, homosexuals, various European ethnic groups, political radicals, many stripes of cultural radicals, and what some called the "youth" culture.[68] The diversity of movements, reform issues, protests, and alternative cultural practices propagated during the 1960s led to "radical cultural disjuncture[s]," which created what many at the time called a "counter culture," which mainstream America believed to be "a barbaric intrusion" and an "invasion of centaurs." Besides a "common enemy" in mainstream WASP American culture and corporate capitalism, there was also a common personalization of political objectives, whereby, to paraphrase the feminist Carol Hanisch, *the personal became political.* What was heretofore assumed to be a "common" American culture, had now fractured along the lines of many distinct, disgruntled, and dissenting counter cultures, each with its own vision and agenda, and each assuming the liberal state would be responsive by expanding the parameters of Civil Rights legislation.[69]

Both the Progressive era and the 1960s Civil Rights reform movements were able to influence and use the federal government as a way to initiate and preserve social changes through the law, enforcement of the law, and federal funding of policy initiatives. However, historians like Alan Dawley have demonstrated that the democratic veneer of the liberal state has also allowed elites to "maintain their rule against popular

---

[67] Matt S. Meier and Feliciano Ribera, *Mexican Americans, American Mexicans: From Conquistadors to Chicanos* (1972; revised, New York: Hill and Wang, 1993): Ch 14-15; Arnoldo De Leon and Richard Griswold del Castillo, *North to Aztlan: A History of Mexican Americans in the United States,* 2nd ed. (1996; revised, Wheeling, IL: Harlan Davidson, 2006): Ch 8.

[68] Eric Foner, *The Story of American Freedom* (New York: Norton, 1998): Ch 12; Cal Jillson, *Pursuing the American Dream: Opportunity and Exclusion over Four Centuries* (Lawrence, KA: University Press of Kansas, 2004); Vine Deloria, Jr., *Spirit and Reason: The Vine Deloria, Jr., Reader* (Golden, CO: Fulcrum Publishing, 1999): Ch 20; Michael Novak, *The Rise of the Unmeltable Ethnics: Politics and Culture in the Seventies* (New York: Macmillan, 1973); Maurice Isserman and Michael Kazin, "The Failure and Success of the New Radicalism," *The Rise and Fall of the New Deal Order, 1930*-1980, Steve Fraser and Gary Gerstle, eds. (Princeton: Princeton University Press, 1989): 212-42. Tom Wolfe: The Electric Kool-Aid Acid Test (1968; reprint, New York: Bantam, 1999).

[69] Theodore Rosak, *The Making of a Counter Culture: Reflections on the Technocratic Society and Its Youthful Opposition* (New York: Anchor Books, 1969): 42-43, 57. I am using Rosak's conception of the "counter culture" in a much broader way than he did in this book (xii, 56, 68). Ruth Rosen, *The World Split Open,* Ibid. 196-97.

discontent" by mediating the seemingly democratic processes of a representative and responsive government. Beneath the surface of elite mediated democratic politics lay "deep structures" of corporate capitalism, racism, sexism, and economic inequality, which have been rarely touched by reformist federal policies. Dawley argued that these deep structures, which have selectively "apportioned" liberty according to one's "class, gender, and race," have never been seriously altered by any 20th century reform movement.

Dawley went on to argue that American liberal elites had devised three "governing strategies" to deal with social change in terms of containing social and economic conflict, and in terms of negotiating the new relationships between "society" and the "state." The older strategy of liberalism (free markets, laissez faire, white supremacy, private property, government by elites) was a staple of the 19th century, but it was not a sufficient governing strategy for modern times (although it would be refurbished in the late 20th century as neo-liberalism). The first new strategy of the early 20th century was progressivism (in broader terms of "government regulation of society in the public interest"). The second was managerial liberalism, which sought to "avoid state bureaucracies by coordinating corporations and other large-scale institutions."[70] The third strategy was New Deal liberalism, which created the welfare state and followed Keynesian economic policies in order to both regulate society and allow corporate control over the economy.[71] The defining "unity" of this historical period (roughly from

---

[70] Alan Dawley, *Struggles for Justice: Social Responsibility and the Liberal State* (Cambridge: Belknap Press of Harvard University Press, 1991). From the perspective of workers, Dawley explained the "corporate rationalization" as "something less than an exercise in pure reason. What the new breed of scientific managers liked to present as a rational system of efficiency and merit nonetheless contained all the irrationalities of class, race, and gender. The supposedly impartial bureaucratic hierarchy was also an axis of unequal power between managers and workers…Rationalization introduced new forms of male dominance" (77-78).

[71] Dawley argued that the New Deal reforms actually "preserved social hierarchy:" "Even as the New Deal responded to popular demands for social justice, it was careful not to infringe too much upon the privileges of wealth…the Roosevelt administration had crafted a compromise between privileged elites and subordinate groups that restrained liberty in the name of security without upending the social order…While the first New Deal tried to save the capitalist system *for* big business, the second tried to save it *from* big business…Although Roosevelt popularized his program with populist rhetoric, the new governing system did not redress the balance of class power or redistribute wealth so much as mediate social antagonisms by creating a new set of bureaucratic institutions. Building on Hoover's initiatives, Roosevelt's New Deal expanded state intervention in the market and launched a welfare state" (385, 394, 395).

the 1890s to the 1930s) was the "persistent efforts of elites to remake the liberal state in the context of the new social forces."[72]

The coherence behind these unifying conceptions of liberal government was "the most potent ideology of all:" nationalism. It was described by many during the early 20th century as a "new nationalism" and its broad based goal was a directed expansion of Americanism through a welfare state and more explicit Americanization initiatives to unite the citizenry and keep them loyal to the state. World War I helped legitimize and spread nationalism and patriotic fervor in order to manufacture the consent of the American people. Nationalism was the most powerful ideological force to create both unity and loyalty in a diverse society, mobilizing the masses, industry, and modern technology for state sponsored projects. Liberal elites used nationalism, reformism, and state interventionism to hold society "together against its own inner contradictions."[73]

Both Dawley and Alan Brinkley have documented the liberal accomodationist and nationalist strategy at work in the New Deal period as well.[74] In "The New Deal and the Idea of the State," Brinkley explored how liberals did not seek to transform the economic structures that created economic injustice, they sought instead to regulate the market and control it through the state, which created the appearance of reform without actually changing the structure of society. However, controlling the market proved a difficult, "unrealistic," and "perhaps even dangerous" intrusion into the economic realm, and besides, many American liberals assumed that progressive reforms and Neal Deal policies had "eliminated the most dangerous features of the capitalist system." The economic boom and triumphant nationalism caused by World War II reinvigorated a return to lassie faire free market policies by

---

[72] Ibid., 31, 62, 64. Dawley further explained his notion of the new models of elite governance: "National elites had to look elsewhere for models of how to govern. In fact, they experimented with three models. The first was old fashioned liberalism – a state of courts and parties, a policy of laissez faire on social issues, the use of troops to police industrial disturbances, and the ruling myths of private property right, separate spheres, and white supremacy. Still the dominant model, it hardly presented an innovative path to the future. The other two models – progressive and managerial – were rival attempts to resolve the contradiction between emerging social forces and the existing liberal state, and they would compete with each other through the First World War into the New Era and all the way to the New Deal. They represented alternative revisions in the American liberal tradition of self-government. Managerial liberals redefined it to mean self-government in industry, emphasizing the public benevolence of the private corporation. Progressives redefined it in social terms, emphasizing government as the benevolent influence balancing the claims of selfish private interests" (163).

[73] Ibid., 1-13, 30-31, 62, 71-73, 105, 114-16, 128-38, 163-65, 175-77, 184-96, 276, 370, 394.

[74] Dawley, Ibid., 370, 385-86, 394.

which many elites thought that unregulated economic growth would create the conditions for social and economic progress, which would then reduce the role of the state to "compensate[ing] for capitalism's inevitable flaws and omissions without interfering with its internal workings."[75] Ira Katznelson argued that this legacy defined the parameters of Johnson's Great Society legislation as well, whereby, the government was used "in unprecedented ways for social ends," but within a compensating framework that did not alter the larger structure of society and the economy. Katznelson also argued that the political climate of the 1960s became more focused on race and cultural pluralism due to the diverse and fractured political movements of various identity groups, and thus, the Great Society programs were seen by many elites to be temporary capitulations to particular groups because of "emergency" situations, not permanent political reforms.[76]

Thus, when the liberal coalition ran out of political capital in the 1970s due to Civil Rights reforms, Great Society reforms, Vietnam, and an unruly counter-cultural movement, it "exploded" and "burst into its constituent shards." A revitalized and powerful conservative reaction co-opted the liberal rhetoric of nationalism and progressive reform in order to orchestrate a conservative rollback of 20th century liberal policies, especially the enlarged and empowered federal government. As Jonathan Rieder notes, no policy was resented more than the effort to "dismantle" the racial "caste system" in America with court orders, federal troops, and enforced integration. Eric Foner noted that many conservatives saw "racial reform [as] being promoted against the will of the democratic majority," who had the right to protect their own interests and to discriminate against those who posed a threat. Anti-Communism, anti-radicalism, and fundamentalist Christianity were also used to refine an older form of patriotism that "demanded a simple, unreflective loyalty." Rieder characterized the conservative backlash as a multifaceted, racist, "proto-fascist revolt of the little man, animated by fearful resentment:" "populism with a vengeance, literally." Widespread discontentment and resentment due to grievances "too varied to be captured in a single category" mobilized large numbers of white working and middle class Americans who were longing for a nostalgic return to a simpler, fairer, whiter, less restrictive, more patriotic, more Christian, and more

---

[75] Alan Brinkley, "The New Deal and the Idea of the State," in *The Rise and Fall of the New Deal Order, 1930*-1980, Steve Fraser and Gary Gerstle, eds. (Princeton: Princeton University Press, 1989): 85-121.

[76] Ira Katznelson, "Was the Great Society a Lost Opportunity?" in *The Rise and Fall of the New Deal Order, 1930*-1980, Steve Fraser and Gary Gerstle, eds. (Princeton: Princeton University Press, 1989): 185-211. Both Katznelson and Alan Dawley place the origins of identity politics to the early 1940's "ethnic pluralism" exemplified in Roosevelt's invocation of a "nation of nations" (*Struggles for Justice*, Ibid., 389).

homogeneous American society. The Republican Party was able to mobilize and unite these fearful Americans, and turn disgruntlement into valuable political capital that was used by Richard Nixon, Ronald Reagan, George H. W. Bush, the Newt Gingrich led congress of 1994, and later George W. Bush. The Republican's overarching policy was to dismantle the New Deal welfare state and initiate reactionary neo-liberal "reforms" (a return to free markets, laissez faire, white/Western supremacy, small/limited government) and national unity/defense (patriotism, WASP culture and values, expanded military-industrial complex).

Conservative reactions and calls for unity often precipitated militant minority reactions and calls for racial and cultural separatism. These rhetorical battles often ignited violent confrontations between radicals and conservatives, between whites and racial minorities, and between racial minorities and law enforcement (the most noticed being the riots of 1965, 1968, and 1992). Liberals who had initiated social change in the 20th century were often associated with the various minority groups who battled against conservatives and law enforcement, and this association "transformed the folk imagery of liberalism" into the poisoned source of conservative angst. Jonathan Rieder argues that America became a "culture of incivility" as "tension" between conservatives and liberals and between conservatives and minority groups turned from impassioned argument to "outright feuding" and "unabashed denunciation."[77] This angry debate would come to be called a "culture war" and the reactionary conservative rhetoric seemed to define the parameters of this war of words. Eric Foner noted that by the 1990s "virtually no politician would admit to being a liberal," while "conservative assumptions" about the benefits of the free market, the evils of "big government," and the unquestioned good of conservative values (like the family, national unity, and patriotism) were taken for granted in public discourse as gospel truths. Conservatives began using their political capital and rhetorical appeal to attack not only the liberal welfare state, but more visibly the symbols of liberal decadence and national decline: funding for the arts and humanities, the national public school curriculum and curricular standards, and the decline of higher education due to multicultural policies.[78]

---

[77] Jonathan Rieder, "The Rise of the 'Silent Majority,'" in *The Rise and Fall of the New Deal Order, 1930-1980*, Steve Fraser and Gary Gerstle, eds. (Princeton: Princeton University Press, 1989): 243-68; Eric Foner, *The Story of American Freedom*, Ibid., Ch 13; Cal Jillson, *Pursuing the American Dream: Opportunity and Exclusion over Four Centuries*, Ibid., Ch 8

[78] Richard Jensen, "The Culture Wars, 1965-1995: A Historian's Map," *Journal of Social History* 29 (Oct 1995): 17-37.

A Rhetoric of Debate:
Towards a Sociology of American Culture Wars

In the midst of the cultural wars, some academics (with mostly liberal sympathies to be sure) were more interested in understanding the nature of the conflict and how both sides might be brought into a more socially productive exchange. In 1991 James Davison Hunter published *Culture Wars: The Struggle to Define America.*[79] At the time this book was the most comprehensive sociological and historical treatment of America's culture wars. Hunter's objective was to sort through the charges and accusations on both sides of the debate in order to come to a sociological understanding of why the culture war was taking place and, further, to draw conclusions about what the culture war meant for American society, institutions, and politics.

According to Hunter, the cultural war[80] was a root a moral debate over "what is fundamentally right and wrong about the world we live in – about what is ultimately good and what is finally intolerable in our communities:" "At stake is how we as Americans will order our lives together." It was a debate over "national identity," the very "meaning of America," and perhaps more importantly "who we, as a nation, will aspire to become." Many of the participants in the cultural war were sincere and "reasonable" people who felt themselves "thrust into controversy" because their "moral commitments," their "bases of moral authority," and their "world views" "compelled" them to defend fundamental truths they held dear. For most participants and viewers of the debate, all knowledge of the issues, the participants, and the war itself were filtered through the various mass media, which by their very forms are highly limited in their coverage and overly focused on the "personalities and events of the moment." Hunter explained that the

---

[79] James Davison Hunter, *Culture Wars: The Struggle To Define America* (New York: Basic Books, 1991). See also, James Davison Hunter, "The Discourse of Negation and the Ironies of Common Culture," *Hedgehog Review* 6:3 (Fall 2004): 24-38.
[80] Hunter has also indicated the much larger issue at stake that transcends the American and contemporary context. He has taken a position at odds with the homogenizing conception of culture made by cultural anthropologists like Clifford Geertz. Hunter has argued, "Culture is, *by its very constitution*, contested....always and everywhere, even when it appears most homogeneous...Where there is culture, there is struggle" [author's emphasis]. Culture is often a battle over who has "the power to project one's vision of the world as the dominant, if not *the only* vision of the world." The creation of "law" or public "policy" is to "create and sustain a normative universe...it is, in short, to take sides on the matter of the public good." James Davison Hunter, "Culture Wars Revisited," *Insight* 10, Institute for Advanced Studies in Culture and Center for Religion and Democracy (Spring 2004): 5-6.

deeply "personal disagreements that fire the culture war were deep and perhaps un-reconcilable." But he also suggested that *these differences are often intensified and aggravated by the way they are presented in public.*[81]

Hunter traced the historical roots of the culture war to the presence of "various minority cultures" (based on religion, sexuality, and race) that have confronted and competed with a "Protestant-based populism" for control over definitions of American "social reality." Over the last two centuries of U.S. history there has been a general "expansion of cultural tolerance" that has accompanied the "slow but steady expansion" of "political and ideological tolerance," "racial tolerance," and "sexual tolerance." One of the most dynamic transformations has been the recent emergence of the "Judeo-Christian consensus" in the 20th century. However, Hunter argued that this consensus was "collapsing" because of a broader "expansion of pluralism," which included many communities beyond the ideological boundaries of the Judeo-Christian worldview (secularists, non-Judeo-Christian religions, feminists, and homosexuals). Hunter explained that "tension" between religious, racial, and ideological groups has always existed in various degrees and will mostly likely never subside because "cultural conflict"[82] continues to evolve "along new and in many ways unfamiliar lines," and because competing ideological and moral visions are rarely "coherent, clearly articulated, sharply differentiate world views."[83] Hunter simplified the culture war into a broad, polarized debate between "the orthodox"

---

[81] Ibid., 31-34, 42-43, 49-51. Davison argued that due to the nature of broadcast media, the culture war is oversimplified and represented as "more polarized than the American public itself...The polarization of contemporary public discussion is in fact intensified by and institutionalized through the very media by which that discussion takes place...Middling positions and the nuances of moral commitment, then, get played into the grid of opposing rhetorical extremes" (159-61). See also: Karlyn Kohrs Campbell, "Marketing Public Discourse," *Hedgehog Review* 6:3 (Fall 2004): 39-54.

[82] Hunter defined "cultural conflict" as the "political and social hostility rooted in different systems of moral understanding. The end to which these hostilities tend is the domination of one cultural and moral ethos over all others." These "systems of moral understanding" are "not merely attitudes that can change on a whim but basic commitments and beliefs that provide a source of identity, purpose, and togetherness for the people who live by them. It is for precisely this reason that political action rooted in these principles and ideals tends to be so passionate." Hunter argued that older forms of cultural conflict have given way to a larger clash between "worldviews:" competing groups are battling over "our most fundamental and cherished assumptions about how to order our lives – our own lives and our lives together in this society. Our most fundamental ideas about who we are as Americana are now at odds" (42). At root, Hunter argued, "cultural conflict is ultimately about the struggle for domination...[it] is about power – a struggle to achieve or maintain the power to define reality" (52). When a dominant group secures and exercises this power over sub-groups it is called "cultural hegemony" (57).

[83] Hunter argued that "the significant divisions on public issues are no longer defined by the distinct traditions of creed, religious observance, or ecclesiastical politics" (105).

(cultural conservatives) and "the progressive" (liberal or libertarians).[84] The debate was over whose culture will "dominate" and, thereby, who will have the "power to define reality." Because the debate focused on competing definitions of reality, it was by its nature a highly *symbolic* war where competing symbols were used to define and legitimate different practices, ideals, and virtues in the public realm. This war over symbols has taken place on various battlefields: the family, education, media and the arts, law, and electoral politics.[85] At the heart of this symbolic war were competing "moral visions" of American history, American identity, and American freedom – all based on competing sources of "moral authority." The orthodox Americans saw America as the embodiment of Judeo-Christian Providence, exceptionalism, and destiny. To them American liberty is based on righteousness and all personal and economic freedom is based on the bounty and grace of God as documented in the sacred text of the *Bible*. Progressives place faith in human reason and social responsibility, and they place moral authority in the rule of law, philosophical principles, and democratic politics – both of which are "living" and malleable human creations that "must evolve as society evolves and matures." To progressives, American liberty is the freedom from all constraints (under the conditions of liberal philosophies set by John Stuart Mill and Charles Taylor) based on the political rights of individuals. Because of the deep ideological and moral divide based on competing moral authorities and expressed in different "moral languages," Hunter argued, "In the final analysis, each side of the cultural divide can only talk past the other" because "what both sides bring to this public debate is, at least consciously, non-negotiable."[86]

Hunter basically agreed with Pat Buchanan that fundamentally the culture wars were a religious war because "what is ultimately at issue are different conceptions of the sacred." But unlike Buchanan (who took up arms to defend his group in the war), Hunter asked a question: Can the American republic survive without a "common agreement as to what constitutes the 'good'" because without such an agreement, "all that remains are competing interests, the power to promote those interests, and the ideological constructions to legitimate those interests?" Hunter

---

[84] Hunter defined "orthodoxy" as "the commitment on the part of adherents to an external, definable, and transcendent authority," which clearly defines "a consistent, unchangeable measure of value, purpose, goodness, and identity." He defined "progressivism" as a "modern" world view built from "a spirit of rationalism and subjectivism:" "Truth tends to be viewed as a process, as a reality that is ever unfolding," and thus, progressives adapt and "re-symbolize historic faiths according to the prevailing assumptions of contemporary life" (44-45).

[85] Ibid., 173-291. Hunter devoted a chapter to each one of these cultural battlefields.

[86] Ibid., 67-106, 39-43, 52-55, 107-32.

argued, no, some common ground must be found. He put forth the possibility of a "new, common rationality, a new *unum* wherein public virtue and public civility can be revitalized." But to achieve common ground, Hunter argued, Americans must first come to an agreement over "*how* to publicly disagree," i.e. formalizing disagreement within the "virtues" of an "authentic" democratic debate. And from there, he argued, Americans must come to terms with a "principled pluralism" and a "principled toleration" with which to guide future negotiation over the parameters of a deeply divided American culture.[87]

A year later Gerald Graff published his award winning[88] *Beyond the Culture Wars: How Teaching the Conflicts Can Revitalize American Education* (1992). Graff's book tried to outline the very techniques and virtues of authentic democratic debate in an effort to encourage people to really engage the debate through listing to their opponents. He argued that too many Americans were sheltered in their own ideological cocoons, and thus, were shut out from opposing points of view. Because of a heightened sense ideological warfare, many Americans adopted a siege mentality by which they withdrew into safe intellectual communities, but this was creating a dangerous "communicative disorder:" "a good deal of American life is organized so as to protect us from having to confront those unpleasant adversaries who may be just the ones we need to listen to." Graff attempted to address and understand some heated debates within his own field (literary studies) in order to find a common ground that can only be gained through an honest appraisal of the merits and limitations of both sides of the debate. His technique was also a pedagogical demonstration of how the culture wars can be taught in classrooms as a way to both understand and defuse the tensions produced by competing points of view.[89]

Graff chastised many conservative critics for their "apocalyptic posturing" and their refusal to see opponents' positions as "legitimate" and "worthy of debate." Graff also took conservative critics to task for their "degree of exaggeration, patent falsehood, and plain hysteria," which boiled down to a "simple fear of change." For instance, Graff singled out the prominent critic Dinesh D'Souza whose *Illiberal Education: The Politics of Race and Sex on Campus* (1991) claimed that universities were "expelling" and "stripping" away all the old liberal arts

---

[87] Ibid., 106, 312-14, 318, 325.
[88] Winner of the 1993 American Book Award.
[89] Gerald Graff, *Beyond the Culture Wars: How Teaching the Conflicts Can Revitalize American Education* (New York: W. W. Norton, 1992): viii. Graff characterized his teaching-the-conflicts model as a way to turn "the poisonous divisions of the culture war into educationally valuable discussion" (62). Graff's technique is a way to teach "critical literacy," which he used Mike Rose's *Lives on the Boundary* (1989) to define as, "framing an argument or taking someone else's argument apart, systematically inspecting a document, an issue, or an event, synthesizing different points of view, applying a theory to disparate phenomena, and so on" (91).

classics to make way for new multicultural texts. Through a close examination of the actual state of university reading lists, Graff pointed out that this claim and its various offspring were based on "recycled evidence" that was "wildly inflated," "grossly exaggerated," and "provably false." Graff concluded, "To put it simply, the critics have not been telling the truth." What was actually happening to the literary canon was a process of change by "accretion at the margins," which had been going on for at least a century or more. Graff argued that the "caricaturing practice" and "political polemics" of conservative critics "obscured the fact that virtually every major advance in humanistic scholarship over the last three decades is indebted to the movements that are widely accused of subverting scholarly values." Graff was not saying that every new theory or academic school of thought delivers an unquestionable truth, but he did argue that new perspectives should be welcomed and honestly evaluated to see if they can expand the boundaries of and add to human knowledge. Graff used the example of Chinua Achebe's critical reading of Joseph Conrad's famous conical work *Heart of Darkness*. While Graff does not completely agree with Achebe's criticism, Graff does admit that Achebe has a good point, which stems from Achebe's different but valid cultural perspective. In Graff's classroom, he does not present one reading of Conrad's novel as *the true* interpretation, but instead teaches the novel "as part of a critical debate about how to read it, which in turn is part of a larger theoretical debate about how politics and power affect the way we read literature."[90] Graff's technique acknowledges and investigates some of the debates at the heart of the cultural war in an effort to legitimize the very real conflict that does exist in America and, thereby, teach his students to democratically debate the issues as "a debate, not a monologue" through an examination of multiple perspectives. Graff argued, "I think frank discussion of these conflicts is more likely to improve our handling of them than pretending they do not exist."[91]

Graff argued that America's system of education was put into a tough position with the culture wars. Many people, especially conservatives, viewed education as a "conflict-free" and value neutral tradition. However, as Graff pointed out, education has always been effected by the conflicts of the wider culture, especially higher education,

---

[90] Graff argued that "literature is a social product, enmeshed in a system of more mundane cultural assumptions, texts, and 'discourses,' not an autonomous creation springing full-blown from the brain of an unconditioned genius. The jargon [of a literary theory]is a way of shifting attention to the 'cultural work' done by the text, suggesting that the text does not stand above its culture but acts on and is acted on by it. It points to the conflicts, contradictions, and struggles in works of literature rather than the unifying elements" (79).
[91] Ibid., 3-5, 8, 16-36.

which in the 20th century has had the "deeply contradictory mission" of both preserving honored traditions while also producing new knowledge by questioning those very traditions. The educational system has reflected changes due not only to the "democratization of culture" produced by the counter-cultures of the 1960s, but also due to advancement of knowledge produced by the structure of the academy. Graff argued that the boundaries of a culture and the frontiers of knowledge have always been contested and debated. Many conservative critics talk of a "consensus" or a "common culture" as if "it were already finished and completed, something that people just 'affirm' or don't affirm rather than something people struggle to create through democratic discussion." The 1960s did not create "divisiveness and difference" in America. Multiple cultures have always been a part of the landscape. Graff argued that the culture war boils down to the very stuff that democracies are made of: a diverse "common discussion" over the public good and public policy. Thus, Graff framed his solution in terms of understanding, realizing, and practicing an inclusive democracy: "We need to distinguish between a shared body of national beliefs, which democracies can do nicely without, and a common national debate about our many differences, which we now need more than ever...[multiculturalists] are not rejecting the idea of a common culture so much as asking for a greater voice in defining it."[92]

Michael Kazin and Joseph A. McCartin have tried to point scholars in the direction of Americanism. The nationalist ideology of Americanism is not only "vast" and "protean," but "famously contested."[93] In a broad sense Americanism represents both a "distinctive" socio-political identity of U.S. citizens and also a particular brand of "loyalty" to the American nation. More particularly Americanism is a "bundle of ideals" with "shifting content" that has "always" been fought over; however, the parameters of Americanism seem to roughly cohere due to a civic foundation of "shared political ideas." Kazin and McCartin claim that the concept of Americanism dates back to the first European settlements. John Winthrop's "city upon a hill," John Adams' invocation of "Providence," and Tom Paine's notion of America as "an asylum for mankind" all represent a particular redemptive and exceptional conception of America and its socio-political ethos. Since then Americans "has been put to a variety of uses, benign and belligerent, democratic and demagogic," and while Americanism is often most associated with more conservative forms of nationalism and

---

[92] Ibid., 6-8, 44-46.
[93] Michael Kazin & Joseph A. McCartin, "Introduction," In *Americanism: New Perspectives on the History of an Ideal*, Michael Kazin & Joseph A. McCartin, eds. (Chapel Hill: The University of North Carolina Press, 2006): 1-21.

patriotism in the service of protecting the status quo, it also contains a "vital countertradition" of dissent.

Historians like David Hollinger have argued that scholars must understand and deal with Americanism because it has become "the most successful nationalist project in all of modern history." Kazin and McCartin argue that Americanism must be studied on "its own terms" so as to understand it as a "well-developed, internally persuasive ideology" and, thereby, "concerned" citizens could shape it towards "more benevolent" ends by "learning how to speak effectively within its idioms." Ultimately Kazin and McCartin suggest that "the ideals of Americanism" could be the "foundation of a new kind of progressive politics" – a politics where the left can "speak convincingly to their fellow citizens" and thus "pose convincing alternatives for the nation as a whole." While thoughtful scholars like Martha Nussbaum have argued that patriotism and nationalism are "morally dangerous," Kazin and McCartin argue that nationalism is a fixture of the modern world and thus "instead of raging against their persistence, we should view them empathetically, doing what we can to help realize the best rather than the worst possibilities of faith in a country and its people…we must do more than rail against patriotic ideals and symbols. For to do so is to wage a losing battle…progressives should claim, without pretense or apology, an honorable place in the long line of those who have demanded that Americanism apply to all and have opposed the efforts of those who have tried to reserve its use for privileged groups and belligerent causes."

Understanding and subscribing to a shared concept of Americanism implies a sense of national identity, but it does so more in terms of *place* and *procedure* than ideology. Americanism is an ambiguous and conflicting bundle of attitudes and ideological commitments, and it holds within it's diversity a common commitment to a shared sacred ground. America as a social, political, cultural, and economic territory is the ground over which various American parties have physically and ideologically wrestled over for centuries. Americanism is not an identifiable ideology per se, but it is the identification of an individual or group as "American" in order to stake one's territorial right for freedom, opportunity, and justice. Thus, as I mentioned in the introduction, America is in essence an institutionalized debate wherein Americans have verbally and physically fought over what America is and should be. Given the complex dynamics of the history of human society and the ecological flux of the natural world, I don't think that there has ever been a stable, unified, or traditional notion of Americanism. I don't agree with much of what Crevecoeur wrote, but I do think he was right when he said that America produced a "surprising metamorphosis." Crevecoeur invoked the notions of *patria* and *alma mater* as a way of saying that America was the sum of its individuals interacting with the land and producing a nation through their work, their conflict, and their claims of "consequence."[94] In this sense the creation of an American nation is the compound and conflicting interaction of diverse parties staking their claim to a single territory. Not all parties have been equally powerful, just, successful, or free, but all parties have verbally and physically struggled with the land and its enhabitants to survive, and in surviving laying a claim of consequence in this nation as one of its own.

Thus, as I mentioned earlier, the disagreement over national identity (What is America, and who is an American?) is the true essence that unites all Americans. An American is one who stakes claim of consequence *in America* and contributes their voice and their demands to the never ending debate over Americanism. There will always be diversity and calls for unity. There will always be culture wars and disagreement. The hope of Americans, if hope is to be found, lies in what the philosopher, linguist, and literary critic Kenneth Burke once called *Ad Bellum Purificandum* – "Towards the Purification of War." By this phrase Burke meant to direct attention to language as the "critical moment" at which human motives take form. Burke argued that a purification of the human ability (and need) to articulate identity, ideology, and purpose into language would be a great help in developing personal agency and social cooperation.[95] It seems to me that while the debate over national identity and purpose can never be resolved, there is the possibility that the method of debate – the tools of discussion and deliberation – might themselves be perfected, as Burke maintained, and thereby, if we as Americans cannot erase our disagreement, we may learn to more productively and peacefully disagree.

---

[94] Crevecoeur, *Letters form an American* Farmer, Ibid., 43-44.
[95] Kenneth Burke, *A Grammar of Motives* (1945; reprint, Berkeley: University of California Press, 1969): 318-20.

II

Americanization:
Historiography of a Concept,
Social Movement, and Practice

Americanization:
Historiography of a Concept, Social Movement, and Practice

While the use of the term "Americanization" has increased in academia, scholarly study of the Americanization movement (1910 – 1920) and specific Americanization practices have been largely neglected, especially by historians. There was a flood of writing on the subject during the first couple decades of the 20th century as it became one of the dominant political discourses of the time. Industrial, government, and education policy makers rushed to create national, state, and local coordinating bodies operating both within and independently of government agencies. A veritable flood of political, educational, and editorial documents filled the popular, scholarly, and government media of the day. There were also several scholarly studies and evaluations of various Americanization efforts, which were conducted from different disciplinary perspectives: educational studies of the development and effectiveness of Americanization programs; political studies of the administrative networks, public policies, and political ramifications of various Americanization initiatives; and there were sociological studies of Americanization as both a socio-political movement and as an socio-cultural phenomenon otherwise labeled as "assimilation" or "acculturation."[96] One important collection of studies was sponsored by the Carnegie Corporation, which commissioned a 10 volume series called *Americanization Studies: The Acculturation of Immigrant Groups Into American Society*. This collection was published from 1920 to 1924 at the cost of some $200,000.[97]

Historical treatment of the Americanization movement, however, was slow in coming. There was some initial treatment by Merle E. Curti in *The Roots of American Loyalty* (1946). Curti's work would later influence his graduate student, Edward G. Hartmann. Hartmann,

---

[96] Herbert A. Miller, *The School and the Immigrant* (Survey Committee of the Cleveland Foundation, 1916); Howard C. Hill, "The Americanization Movement," *American Journal of Sociology*, XXIV (May 1919): 609-627; Isaac B. Berkson, *Theories of Americanization: A Critical Study with Special Reference to the Jewish Group* (New York: Teachers College Press, 1920); Frank V. Thompson, *Schooling of the* Immigrant, Carnegie Corporation Americanization Studies (New York: Harper & Brothers, 1920).

[97] This series was reissued in toto under the editor William S. Bernard: Publication No. 125, Patterson Smith Reprint Series in Criminology, Law Enforcement, and Social Problems (Montclair: Patterson Smith, 1971). For a review and short history of this series see: Milton M. Gordon, "The American Immigrant Revisited," *Social Forces* 54:2 (Dec 1975): 470-74.

under the direction of Curti, wrote *The Movement to Americanize the Immigrant* in 1948.[98] Hartmann's book would become the definitive history of the Americanization movement, and it remains to this day the best of the few historical monographs on the subject.

Hartmann's rather narrow focus chronicled the rise of private reform and educational policy organizations who were concerned about the assimilation of the immigrant during the first decade and a half of the 20th century. These reformers were able to influence the Bureau of Naturalization and the Bureau of Education in order to create formal governmental agencies to oversee and coordinate state and local Americanization initiatives, organize Americanization conferences, and also supply posters, pamphlets, and textbooks. This "social movement" or "crusade" began as a "positive program" of education to meet the "problem" of immigration in the U.S. and it reached its pinnacle in the years 1915-16 as the U.S. geared toward entry into the war. But a national hysteria concerning foreigners and anti-Americanism swept the country during and after the war up until 1920, which created more a "negative," fearful, and coercive focus to Americanization initiatives. It was also during this time, specifically in 1919, that federal funding for Americanization efforts were cut back, which caused the Bureau of Education to discontinue Americanization activities, and which left the Bureau of Naturalization as the sole federal body in charge of Americanization programs. The Bureau of Naturalization's activities were confined primarily to creating and distributing published materials (including textbooks), monitoring local Americanization activities, and working with the public schools to incorporate Americanization programs in the standard national curriculum. It was also during 1918-21 that Americanization efforts became more professionalized through academic departments of education and sociology, and Americanization was grafted as one plank in a broader public school initiative of creating an adult educational system, which Hartmann argued was perhaps the greatest legacy of the movement. The ideology of "Americanism" (and its various rhetorical forms) was rarely defined by reformers except in terms of the foreigner leaving behind the old ways in order to adopt a vague American identity. Hartmann argued that this lack of definition underscored a cultural common identity shared by reformers and their audience, whereby, the "mission" of Americanization and the values of Americanism where taken for granted as self-evident norms, and thus, Hartmann compared it to other idealistic national "crusades" like abolitionism, woman's suffrage, civil service reform, and the common school movement.[99]

---

[98] Edward George Hartmann, *The Movement to Americanize the Immigrant* (1948; reprint, New York: AMS Press, 1967).
[99] Hartmann, Ibid., 236, 252-53, 261-70.

The next historical treatment of the subject was published via a chapter in John Higham's superb book on U.S. nativism and nationalism, *Strangers in the Land* (1955).[100] Higham discussed how the broader currents of xenophobia, nativism, and nationalism during the 1890s concealed into a rampant and rabid nationalist crusade of "America for Americans" and "100 per cent Americanism" during and after World War I. Fear of the foreigner gave way to a more ambiguous fear of "disloyalty," "the gravest sin in the morality of nationalism," which was any thought that might question the "Absolute and Unqualified Loyalty to Our Country." This search for disloyalty focused uncomfortably on "hyphenated Americans" (German-Americans in particular) and their ability to support not only the war effort, but the greater cause of American nationalism. Infusing the search for disloyalty was a "positive and prescriptive" rhetorical abstraction that did not rise "to the dignity of a systematic doctrine:" "100 per cent Americanism." While there was no specific dogmatic or programmatic ritual to prove one's "Americanism," there were several assumptions underlying this phrase. One was a "belligerent" demand for "universal conformity" to the "spirit of nationalism" and total national loyalty" to the State, which was regulated through "the pressure of collective judgment." It was during 1917 that "The American's Creed" ("I pledge allegiance to the flag...") was introduced as a classroom ritual in public schools to remind children of the object of their loyalty, but more so to rhetorically instill the virtue of "right-thinking, i.e. the enthusiastic cultivation of obedience and conformity." 100 per cent Americanism, as Higham argued, was primarily a rhetorical affair of "propaganda" and "exhortation," but with the onset of the war nationalists supported the expansion of state powers and "the punitive and coercive powers" of the state to support if not mandate loyalty and conformity.[101]

The work of Higham and Hartmann are still the definitive historical treatments of Americanization and the Americanization movement, but neither one of them bothered to historically analyze or reconstruct actual Americanization programs at the micro level of local and institutional practice. There have been few scholarly treatments since Hartmann and Higham that have revisited the Americanization movement, and fewer yet that have conducted original analysis of the extensive primary documents on either federal, state, local or institutional levels.[102] There have been no books or scholarly monographs on the subject of the Americanization movement since 1948, and Hartmann and

---

[100] John Higham, *Strangers in the Land: Patterns of American Nativism, 1860-1925* (1955; reprint, New Brunswick: Rutgers University Press, 1998).
[101] Higham, ibid., 196, 200, 204-05.
[102] See footnote 19.

Higham remain to this day the most cited references in relation to this subject. By the 1960s and 70s there was a rise of scholarly activity on numerous subjects related to the concept of Americanization, the Americanization movement, or various types of Americanization practices and programs. But in order to find this literature researchers must range over many academic disciplines and disciplinary fields of study, and one finds mostly fragmented and narrow treatments that have little if any connection beyond disciplinary discourses.

There is one monograph of note during this time that must be mentioned because it has gained a reputation in the literature. Robert A. Carlson's *The Quest for Conformity: Americanization through Education* (1975; revised and expanded in 1987) was a somewhat influential study and it has been moderately cited by various scholars. [103] However, its reputation is somewhat baffling because this book is severely flawed as a work of scholarship. For one, Carlson's title is misleading because the book is not really about education. It is a revisionist history of Americanization as a broader form of cultural indoctrination. Although the book does discuss education throughout, it is highly generalized and it does not actually analyze educational processes per se except in noting that cultural indoctrination was conducted through schools and other educational forms. The whole book suffers from a penchant for overgeneralization (many intricate topics get rushed over in a few paragraphs), and in light of Hartmann's and Higham's work, Carlson's book has nothing really to offer except its theoretical framework. Carlson's book is really the only work to fully contextualize Americanization within the full scope of American history, and thereby, argue that "Americanization" has been a central preoccupation of political and cultural leaders. But his basic argument consists of condemning all Americanizers as agents of "cultural genocide." In Carlson's formulation, Americanization (and seemingly the whole of U.S. educational history) was nothing but a "policy of genocide of non-Caucasians." Carlson's thesis is an over-generalized, and in light of further contemporary scholarship, false, structural account of U.S. history positing a singular and monolithic WASP society "Americanizing" non-whites via a one-way process of cultural imperialism. [104]

---

[103] Robert A. Carlson, *The Quest for Conformity: Americanization through Education* (New York: John Wiley and Sons, 1975). Carlson expanded this book somewhat into a more general treatment of Americanization as a whole: *The Americanization Syndrome: A Quest for Conformity* (New York: St. Martin's Press, 1987). However, the later book is essentially the same work with the same basic portrait and relying on the same basic secondary and primary source material. See John W. Briggs, review of *The Quest for Conformity*, by Robert A. Carlson, *History of Education Quarterly* 28:4 (Winter 1988): 689-91.
[104] Carlson, ibid., 12, 15, 93, 141.

Carlson's work highlights an important problematic within the literature on Americanization. The very term "Americanization" has always been, and continues to be, substantially ambiguous. It is akin to other widely used socio-political slogans like "republican," "progressive," or "liberal."[105] Most historians have treated the term "Americanization" as synonymous with the assimilation or integration of immigrants into mainstream American socio-political culture. Richard Hofstadter offhandedly linked "naturalization and Americanization" in his work on the progressive era.[106] Alan Kraut broadly situated the term "Americanization" as an "ideology of mobility" permeating discussions of both cultural assimilation and specific forms of socialization via the institution of schooling.[107] Kraut's use of "Americanization" signified the gradual and conflicting process (the "cultural tug of war") of assimilating the immigrant within American society. Kraut's broad usage is representative of the majority of scholars in history, literature, and the

---

[105] For discussions of the term "republicanism" see: Linda K. Kerber, "The Republican Ideology of the Revolutionary Generation," *American Quarterly* 37 (Autumn 1985): 474-495; Joyce Appleby, "Republicanism and Ideology," *American Quarterly* 37 (Autumn 1985): 461-473; Daniel T. Rodgers, "Republicanism: The Career of a Concept," *The Journal of American History* 79 (June 1992): 11-38. For a discussion of the term "progressivism" see: John D. Buenker, John C. Burnham, and Robert M. Crunden, *Progressivism* (Cambridge, MA: Schenkman Publishing Company, Inc., 1977); Daniel T. Rodgers, "In Search of Progressivism," *Reviews in American History* 10 (Dec 1982), 113-132; Arthur S. Link and Richard L. McCormick, *Progressivism* (Wheeling, IL: Harlan Davidson, Inc., 1983); James T. Kloppenberg, *Uncertain Victory: Social Democracy and Progressivism in European and American Thought, 1870 – 1920* (Oxford: Oxford University Press, 1986); John Whiteclay Chambers II, *The Tyranny of Change: American in the Progressive Era, 1890 – 1920* (1992; reprint, New Brunswick, NJ: Rutgers University Press, 2000); Alan Dawley, *Struggles for Justice: Social Responsibility and the Liberal State* (Cambridge: Belknap Press of Harvard University Press, 1991). For a discussion of the term "liberalism" see: Gary Gerstle, "The Protean Character of American Liberalism," *The American Historical Review* 99:4 (Oct 1994): 1043-1073; James T. Kloppenberg, *Uncertain Victory: Social Democracy and Progressivism in European and American Thought, 1870 – 1920* (Oxford: Oxford University Press, 1986); James T. Kloppenberg, *The Virtues of Liberalism* (Oxford: Oxford University Press, 1998).
[106] Richard Hofstadter, *The Age of Reform: From Bryan to F.D.R.* (New York: Vintage Books, 1955), 181.
[107] Historians have also focused on other cultural media, which socialized immigrants. Jackson Lears described how "ethnocentrism reinforced professionalism" in the advertising business and how advertisements as medium of "manipulation" and "control" "showed recent immigrants how to assimilate to 'American' ways." *Fables of Abundance: A Cultural History of Advertising in America* (New York: Basic Books, 1994), 205, 253. Eric Foner noted, "The department store, dance hall, and motion picture theater were as much agents of Americanization as the school and workplace. Eric Foner, *The Story of American Freedom* (New York: W. W. Norton & Co., 1998), 191. See also Rob Kroes, "American Empire and Cultural Imperialism: A View from the Receiving End," *Rethinking American History in a Global Age*, Thomas Bender, ed. (Berkeley: University of California Press, 2002): 295-313.
Lawrence Cremin also focused on several educative media during the early 20th century. "Media of Popular Communication," *American Education: The Metropolitan Experience, 1876-1980* (New York: Harper & Row, 1988), 322-72.

social sciences.[108] Since the mid 1990s historians and social scientists have also acknowledged Americanization-as-assimilation as a racialized process imbued with white supremacy. David Roediger has argued, "The process of Americanizing European immigrants acquired a sense of whiteness and of white supremacy," and thus, there was a general conflation of "whiteness with Americanism."[109]

Gary Gerstle's "Liberty, Coercion, and the Making of Americans" (1997) traced out the origins of the Americanization-as-assimilation concept all the way back to the 18th century French-American farmer, J. Hector St John De Crevecoeur.[110] Gerstle argued that Crevecoeur's conception of assimilation in *Letters from an American Farmer* (1782) was one of the "most influential mediations on what it means to become an American." Not only did the Crevecoeurian myth help define the early 20th century ideal of the "melting pot," but it also influenced the way 20th century sociologists and historians conceptualized theories of assimilation (often using the term "Americanization"), which in tern had an influence on public policy and national debates.

Crevecoeur's conception of Americanization pervaded the work of Robert E. Park and the Chicago school sociologists, but this school also criticized one part of the myth: the notion that assimilation was quick and easy. Their work took place during a general "recoil" of liberal social scientists disturbed by the "reaction and intolerance" of the Americanization drives during World War I and the Red Scare. Because the term Americanization gained such "a bad, nativist odor" after the war, it was dropped from the vocabulary of many liberal reformers and social scientists. Many social scientists also began to believe that immigrant cultures were "resistant to assimilation," which meant "no magical fusing" of cultures via the melting pot was taking place. The work of Oscar Handlin was a product of this critical environment, and he would serve as an important transitional figure leading to the eventual dismantling of the Crevecoeurian assimilationist theory by the "new" immigrant historians of the 1960s and 70s (Frank Thistlewaite, Rudolph J. Vecoli, and Herbert Gutmann). However, some scholars have been charged with "resurrecting" parts of the Crevecoeurian myth, such as

---

[108] Alan M. Kraut, *The Huddled Masses: The Immigrant in American Society, 1880 – 1921*, 2nd ed. (1982; reprint, Wheeling: Harlan Davidson, Inc., 2001), 120, 125, 128-29, 155.
[109] David R. Roediger, *Towards the Abolition of Whiteness* (1994; reprint, London: Verso, 2000), 187-90; David R. Roediger, *Working Toward Whiteness: How America's Immigrants Became White* (New York: Basic Books, 2005), 84-85, 91, 143.
[110] Gary Gerstle, "Liberty, Coercion, and the Making of Americans," *The Journal of American History* 84:2 (Sept 1997): 524-58; J. Hector St John De Crevecoeur, *Letters from an American Farmer* (1782; reprint, Oxford: Oxford University Press).

assimilation's "emancipatory impulse."[111]

Invoking radical scholars of the 1960s and the new scholarship of David R. Roediger and others, Gerstle criticized neo-Crevecoeurian scholars for not focusing enough on the complexity and constraints (class, gender, race, nation) of the Americanization process by which "social forces external to the immigrant" play a very significant, if not the most significant, role in the Americanization of immigrants. Gerstle argued that "structure[s] of power" limited the options (and also often coerced) immigrants during the assimilation/Americanization process. He reviewed the work of more critical "new" immigrant scholars (like Gutmann, Vecoli, Hoerder, Bodnar, Morawska, and Gabaccia) who viewed Americanism as a "cultural strategy" deployed by the wealthy and powerful (employers, natives, ethnic middle-class allies) to "augment" their privileged position. Americanization was thus a "surrender" or "capitulation" to "a capitalist order," which could have positive effects for some immigrants (those few who could "make capitalism work for them"), but which had the negative effect for most by way of "acquiescing" in their own "oppression." Gerstle argued: "The elites were intent on becoming Crevecoeurian 'new men'; the masses wanted to remain who they were."

Gerstle also acknowledged the complexity of Americanization because "as indifferent or hostile to America" as immigrants could be, "a majority of the new immigrants stayed" and many of them went on to acquire not only an "American identity," but also a "profound patriotic awakening." Gerstle criticized the overly optimistic accounts make by Fuchs, Sollors and Hollinger who seemed to argue for a theory of personal agency and a fluidness to identity that did not take into account the restrictiveness of structural constraints (especially race). Gerstle argued, "race, even more than class and gender, still limits the options of those who seek to become American." Gerstle clearly believed that "historical circumstances and social structures undermined experiments in the fashioning of identity," and he looked to newer studies on gender and working class Americanism (including his own), which have created a "synthesis between agency and structure" and, thereby, demonstrated

---

[111] Gerstle specifically indicts Lawrence H. Fuchs and Werner Sollors, but Donna R. Gabaccia placed Gerstle in the same camp. Gabaccia argued that Gerstle "remains as much a neo-Crevecoeurian as the scholars he criticizes" because Gerstle approached Crevecoeurian assimilationist theory too much on its "own terms." For instance, Gabaccia points to Gerstle's focus on only Europeans (ignoring other minorities like Blacks, Native Americans, and Latinos), and his focus on the nation state (ignoring transnational and diaspora elements). Gabaccia argued that Gerstle should have extended his critique of assimilation, coercion, structural constraints, and the power of the nation state to include a "critique of national historiography" and "the nation itself." Donna R. Gabaccia, "Liberty, Coercion, and the Making of Immigration Historians," *The Journal of American History* 84:2 (Sept 1997): 570-75.

how "Americanization involves both inventiveness and constraint:" America was not "simply a Crevecoeurian land of possibility," it was also "a land of constraint."

Despite the important social scientific and historical usage of Americanization as a term for *assimilation*, there have been some hidden costs in this terminology. What has been lost is the specific historical *context* in which the term "Americanization" gained its wide currency. Part of the difficulty for a contemporary historian researching the Americanization movement and specific Americanization educational practices is the wide ahistorical usage of the term "Americanization" in a diverse array of studies on immigration, assimilation, nationalism, and cultural socialization.[112] "Americanization" is anything and everything concerned with the social, cultural, and political transformations of individuals and ethnic groups in America. This ambiguous usage has also been revitalized in the late 20th century culture wars and given new currency as either a generalized act of cultural imperialism or an equally generalized act of national solidarity.[113] While the usage of the term in its assimilationist sense is important in order to study U.S. nationalism and conflict over national identity and culture, it has also distracted from if not distorted our knowledge of the historical emergence and evolution of the early 20th century Americanization movement and its specific educational, social, legal, and institutional practices. There is much work to be done on Americanization as a diverse and contradictory "progressive" social movement tied to specific macro historical contexts and micro institutional and individual practices. The Americanization movement and specific Americanization practices have been largely neglected by social scientists and historians over the last fifty years.

---

[112] Milton M. Gordon, *Assimilation in American Life: The Role of Race, Religion, and National Origins* (New York: Oxford University Press, 1964); Nathan Glazer and Daniel Patrick Moynihan, *Beyond the Melting Pot: The Negroes, Puerto Ricans, Jews, Italians, and Irish of New York*, 2nd ed. (1963; reprint, Cambridge: MIT Press, 1974); Nathan Glazer, "Is Assimilation Dead?" *Annals of the American Academy of Political and Social Science* 530 (Nov 1993): 122-36; Russell A. Kazal, "Revisiting Assimilation: The Rise, Fall, and Reappraisal of a Concept in American Ethnic History," *The American Historical Review* 100:2 (Apr 1995): 437-71; Dennis J. Downey, "From Americanization to Multiculturalism: Political Symbols and Struggles for Cultural Diversity in Twentieth-Century American Race Relations," *Sociological Perspectives* 42:2 (Summer 1999): 249-78; For a good sample of this literature see: George E. Pozzetta, ed. *Assimilation, Acculturation, and Social Mobility* (New York: Garland Publishing, 1991).

[113] For liberal condemnation of the term see: Michael Walzer, "What Does it Mean to Be an 'American?'" *Social Research* (1990); Reprinted in Michael Walzer, *What It Means to Be an American: Essays on the American Experience* (New York: Marsilio, 1996). For conservative use of the term see: Arthur M. Schlesinger, Jr., *The Disuniting of America: Reflections on a Multicultural Society*, revised ed. (1991; revised, New York: W. W. Norton, 1998); E. D. Hirsch Jr., "Americanization and the Schools," *The Clearing House* 72:3 (Jan/Feb, 1999): 136-39; Samuel P. Huntington, *Who Are We? The Challenges to America's National Identity* (New York: Simon & Schuster, 2004).

While there has been some very good work done in various areas, almost all scholarship is overly narrow, fragmented, and alienated from the larger body of diverse and disconnected literature.

The most visible scholarship on the Americanization movement is found within the numerous histories and historiographies on the "Progressive Era" of U.S. history. While most historical works on the Progressive era give some treatment of the Americanization movement it is often very briefly and generally mentioned, and sometimes this subject is blurred within a more general discussion (as noted above) of immigration and assimilation.[114] There are many good historical treatments of the Americanization movement in various scholarly articles and in parts of historical books; however, these treatments as noted are fragmented along disciplinary lines and very partial in their accounts. For instance, there have been important political treatments of the Americanization movement in relation to law or the federal

---

[114] There is only book length work on the Progressive era that gives substantial treatment to the Americanization movement: John F. McClymer, *War and Welfare: Social Engineering in America, 1890-1925* (Westport, CT: Greenwood, 1980). McClymer has also published an important article "The Federal Government and the Americanization Movement, 1915-1924" *Prologue: The Journal of the National Archives* 10 (Spring 1978): 23-41. This article was republished along with several other important articles on the Americanization movement in an anthology edited by George E. Pozzetta called *Americanization, Social Control, and Philanthropy* (New York: Garland Publishing, 1991). Gary Gerstle is one of the few historians of 20th century America that has given the Americanization movement extended treatment in several works, especially in *American Crucible: Race and Nation in the Twentieth Century* (Princeton: Princeton University Press, 2001). See also: Desmond King, *Making Americans: Immigration, Race, and the Origins of the Diverse Democracy* (Cambridge: Harvard University Press, 2000). There is a problem, however, with all these fine treatments of the Americanization movement. All of these works rely primarily on the federal archives of the departments of Immigration and Naturalization (Record Group 85, National Archives), Labor (Record Group 174, National Archives), and Education (Record Group 12, National Archives). Thus, the historical treatment of the Americanization movement in these works focuses mostly on the federal level with little or no treatment of state, local, or institutional/organizational levels (although there is often mention of national institutions like the public school system or national organizations like the Daughters of the American Revolution). For a brief discussion of the usage of these federal archives see: Noah Pickus, *True Faith and Allegiance: Immigration and American Civic Nationalism* (Princeton: Princeton University Press, 2005): 206-07, footnote 36. One should also note that most of the literature on the Americanization movement focuses on persons, organizations, and events from the East Coast or Midwest, but there were active Americanization campaigns in the West and Southwest, especially California. Noah Pickus argued incorrectly that "Americanization was primarily an eastern and midwestern phenomenon," which "largely ignored other [non-European] immigrants, such as those from China or Mexico (Ibid., 206, footnote 35). There is a large, but fragmented body of research on the Americanization of peoples from Mexico, Japan, Guam, Philippines, Puerto Rico, Hawaii, and Native Americans. Often this literature links (although rather generally) the Americanization movement to U.S. imperialism. See footnote 26 in this essay.

government.[115] There have been several treatments of the Americanization movement in relation to education, usually elementary education, but sometimes in relation to adult education or more to just educational processes generally.[116] There have also been historical treatments of immigrants and education, which do not directly confront or even mention the Americanization movement.[117] There have been several treatments of the Americanization movement in relation to citizenship or citizenship education.[118] There have been many treatments of the Americanization in relation to economic institutions, like

[115] Kenneth B. O'Brien Jr., "Education, Americanization and the Supreme Court: The 1920's," *American Quarterly* 13:2 (Summer, 1961): 161-171; John F. McClymer, "The Federal Government and the Americanization Movement, 1915-1924" *Prologue: The Journal of the National Archives* 10 (Spring 1978)P 22-41.

[116] Lawrence A. Cremin, *The Transformation of the School: Progressivism in American Education, 1876 – 1957* (New York: Vintage Books, 1961); Robert A. Carlson, "Americanization as an Early Twentieth-Century Adult Education Movement," *History of Education Quarterly* 10:4 (Winter 1970): 440-64; David Tyack, *The One Best System: A History of American Urban Education*, Part 4.4, "Americanization: Match and Mismatch" (Cambridge: Harvard University Press, 1974); Robert A. Carlson, *The Quest for Conformity: Americanization through Education* (New York: John Wiley and Sons, 1975); John F. McClymer, "The Americanization Movement and the Education of the Foreign-Born Adult, 1914-25," In *American Education and the European Immigrant: 1840-1940*, edited by Bernard J. Weiss. Urbana, IL: University of Illinois Press, 1982. Paper originally prepared for 12th annually Duquesne History Forum, Oct. 18-20, 1978; Vincent P. Franklin, "Ethos and Education: The Impact of Educational Activities on Minority Ethnic Identity in the United States," *Review of Research in Education* 10 (1983): 3-21; David Tyack, Thomas James, and Aaron Benavot, "Moral Majorities and the School Curriculum: Making Virtue Mandatory, 1880-1930." *Law and the Shaping of Public Education, 1785-1954* (Madison: University of Wisconsin Press, 1987):154-76; Michael R. Olneck, "Americanization and the Education of Immigrants, 1900-1925: An Analysis of Symbolic Action," *American Journal of Education* 97 (Aug 1989): 398-423.

[117] Michael R. Olneck and Marvin Lazerson, "The School Achievement of Immigrant Children: 1900-1930," *History of Education Quarterly* 14:4 (Winter 1974): 453-82; Raymond A. Mohl, "The International Institutes and Immigrant Education, 1910-40," In *American Education and the European Immigrant: 1840-1940*, edited by Bernard J. Weiss. Urbana, IL: University of Illinois Press, 1982. Paper originally prepared for 12th annually Duquesne History Forum, Oct. 18-20, 1978; Nicholas V. Montalto, "The Intercultural Education Movement, 1924-41: The Growth of Tolerance as a Form of Intolerance," In *American Education and the European Immigrant: 1840-1940*, edited by Bernard J. Weiss. Urbana, IL: University of Illinois Press, 1982. Paper originally prepared for 12th annually Duquesne History Forum, Oct. 18-20, 1978; Nicholas V. Montalto, A History of the Intercultural Education Movement, 1924-1941 (New York: Garland Press, 1982).

[118] Michael Kammen, *A Machine That Would Go of Itself: The Constitution in American Culture* (New York: Vintage Books, 1987): 235-48. Rogers M. Smith, *Civic Ideals: Conflicting Visions of Citizenship in U.S. History* (New Haven: Yale University Press, 1997): Ch 12; Jeffrey Mirel, "Civic Education and Changing Definitions of American Identity, 1900 – 1950," *Educational Review* 54:4 (2002): 143-152. Noah Pickus, *True Faith and Allegiance: Immigration and American Civic Nationalism* (Princeton: Princeton University Press, 2005): Ch 4-6.

businesses, factories, and labor camps.[119] Historians have also explored the Americanization movement in relation to institutions and organizations like Social Settlement houses and the Catholic Church.[120] There have also been many studies of Americanization in relation to gender and minority cultures.[121] This particular literature has seen the

---

[119] Gerd Korman, *Industrialization, Immigrants, and Americanizers: The View from Milwaukee, 1866 – 1921* (Madison: The State Historical Society of Wisconsin, 1967); Stephen Meyer, "Adapting the Immigrant to the Line: Americanization in the Ford Factory, 1914-1921," *Journal of Social History* 14 (1980): 67-82; James R. Barrett, "Americanization from the Bottom Up: Immigration and the Remaking of the Working Class in the United States, 1880 – 1930," *The Journal of American History* 79:3 (Dec 1992): 996-1020; Gilbert G. Gonzalez, "Labor and Community: The Camps of Mexican Citrus Pickers in Southern California," *The Western Historical Quarterly* 22:3 (Aug 1991): 289-312.

[120] Rivka Shpak Lissak, *Pluralism and Progressives: Hull House and the New Immigrants, 1890 – 1919* (Chicago: University of Chicago Press, 1989); Ruth Hutchinson Crocker, *Social Work and Social Order: The Settlement Movement in Two Industrial Cities, 1889 – 1930*; Philip Gleason, "The Catholic Church in American Public Life in the Twentieth Century," *Logos: A Journal of Catholic Thought and Culture* 3:4 (2000): 85-99.

[121] On gender see: Eileen Boris, "Reconstructing the 'Family': Women, Progressive Reform, and the Problem of Social Control," in *Gender, Class, Race and Reform in the Progressive Era*, Noralee Frankel and Nancy S. Dye, eds. (Lexington, KT: The University Press of Kentucky, 1991): 73-86. On Latinos see: George Sanchez, "'Go After the Women:' Americanization and the Mexican Immigrant Woman, 1915 – 1929," *Stanford Center for Chicano Research, Working Paper Series No. 6* (June 1984): 1-32. Revised and reprinted in *Unequal Sisters: A Multi-Cultural Reader in U.S. Women's History*, ed. Ellen Carol DuBois and Vicki L. Ruiz (New York: Routledge, 1990); Reinhard R. Doerries, "The Americanizing of the German Immigrant: A Chapter from U.S. Social History," *American Studies* 23:1 (1978): 51-59; Mario T. Garcia, "Americanization and the Mexican Immigrant, 1880-1930," *Journal of Ethnic Studies* 6:2 (Summer 1978): 19-34; George J. Sanchez, *Becoming Mexican American: Ethnicity, Culture and Identity in Chicano Los Angeles, 1900 – 1945* (Oxford: Oxford University Press, 1993): Ch 4 & 5; Guadalupe San Miguel Jr. and Richard R. Valencia, "From the Treaty of Guadalupe Hidalgo to Hopwood: The Educational Plight and Struggle of Mexican Americans in the Southwest," *Harvard Educational Review* 68:3 (1998): 353-412. On Native Americans see: David Wallace Adams, "Fundamental Considerations: The Deep Meaning of Native American Schooling, 1880 – 1900," *Harvard Educational Review* 58:1 (Feb 1988): 1-28; Michael C. Coleman, *American Indian Children at School, 1850-1930* (Jackson: University Press of Mississippi, 1993); David Wallace Adams, *Education for Extinction: American Indians and the Boarding School Experience, 1875-1923* (Lawrence: University Press of Kansas, 1995); Donal F. Lindsey, *Indians at Hampton Institute, 1877-1923* (Urbana: University of Illinois Press, 1995). On Japanese see: David K. Yoo, *Growing Up Nisei: Race, Generation, and Culture among Japanese Americans of California, 1924-49* (Urbana: University of Illinois Press, 2000). On Puerto Ricans see: Pedro Caban, "Subjects and Immigrants During the Progressive Era," *Discourse* 23:3 (2001): 24-51. On Filipinos see: Anne Paulet, "To Change the World: The Use of American Indian Education in the Philippines," *History of Education Quarterly* 47:2 (May 2007): 173-202. On Hawaiians see: Manette K. P. Benham and Ronald H. Heck, *Culture and Educational Policy in Hawai'i: The Silencing of Native Voices* ()Mahwah, NJ: Lawrence Erlbaum, 1998); C. Kalani Beyer, "The Connection of Samuel Chapman Armstrong as Both Borrower and Architect of Education in Hawai'i," *History of Education Quarterly* 47:1 (Feb 2007): 23-48. On African Americans see: James D. Anderson, *The Education of Blacks in the South, 1860-1935* Chapel Hill: University of North Carolina Press, 1988).

largest growth in the last quarter century, but it also suffers from the most fragmentation as many of these studies are completely isolated from each other and the larger national and international (U.S. Imperialism) Americanization movement(s). And finally Americanization as assimilation as well as the Americanization movement make many appearances in various histories of immigration and histories of ethnic groups in America.[122]

What one learns in this vast and fragmented literature is that there has been little attempt to bridge disciplinary lines or topical studies in order to articulate a full and complex understanding of both Americanization as an international, national, state, and local movement, and also Americanization as a concrete historical practice on the institutional, programmatic, and individual level. Hartmann's seminal treatment, and many other important works since, have focused specifically on national and state level activities with very little attempt to integrate national, state, and local levels together. The Americanization movement was a highly localized affair and, as Hartmann demonstrated, both government and private Americanization agencies on both the national and state levels did their best to coordinate an ungovernable and highly dispersed grassroots movement. Most historical treatments of the Americanization movement either give a monolithic WASP society trying to Americanize various ethnic groups or a highly detailed and localized history of a specific Americanization program with no mention of larger state and national affairs.

Given the resurgence of immigration as a national issue and the armed intervention and social reconstruction of American troop in the Middle East, there needs to be greater awareness and understanding of the Americanization movement and its legacy. But in order to articulate the importance of this subject with the aim of directing further studies, the field desperately needs a synthesis that can tie the myriad studies of the national, state, and local levels to the splintered studies of various "Americanized" ethnic groups and the specific programs of socio-political localities. But before this work can take place there needs to be a systematic search for all the scholarly work done on this historical movement, which is currently buried in various disciplinary and topical niches.

---

[122] Leonard Dinnerstein and David M. Reimers, *Ethnic Americans: A History of Immigration and Assimilation* (New York: New York University Press, 1977); Thomas J. Archdeacon, *Becoming American: An Ethnic History* (New York: The Free Press, 1983); John Bodnar, *The Transplanted: A History of Immigrants in Urban America* (Bloomington: Indiana University Press, 1985); Leonard Dinnerstein and David M. Reimers, *Natives and Strangers: Blacks, Indians, and Immigrants in America* (Oxford: Oxford University Press, 1990); Alan M. Kraut, *The Huddled Masses: The Immigrant in American Society, 1880 – 1921*, 2nd ed. (1982; reprint, Wheeling: Harlan Davidson, Inc., 2001); David R. Roediger, *Working Toward Whiteness: How America's Immigrants Became White* (New York: Basic Books, 2005).

Once some synthetic historiographical and historical works appear, then it will be important to start filling in the gaps of what we don't know. For instance, greater attention needs to be paid to the connection between individual, institutional, local, state, national initiatives, and international initiatives in order to more fully explain how the Americanization movement emerged, "moved," evolved, and transformed educational policy and practice. New studies would also need to incorporate the work of sociologists, political scientists, and psychologists in order to analyze historical data via new social scientific theories. Some of this theoretical work could include conceptions of ideology and nationalism, organizational and state theory, and critical race theories. Social movement theory would be one especially useful tool with which to explain "structures and processes, established and emergent organizations, institutionalized authority, and transgressive contention" as well as the "connections between local or specialized fields and broader societal systems."[123]

Another theoretical framework that would be useful is Kevin J. Doughtery's relative autonomy of the state theory, which argues that state officials (including educational administrators and teachers) had their own agendas that were "relatively autonomous" of interest group pressure (business, foundations, professional organizations, and popular coalitions), but were also influenced indirectly and directly by these interest groups through resource dependence and ideology.[124] Using Doughtery's theory, a historian could demonstrate how national and state organizations propagated potent nationalist and cultural ideologies of Americanism and offers of financial support for local Americanization initiatives, while as the same time demonstrate the "relatively autonomous" decisions and programs actually conducted by educational administrators, teacher training programs, and individual teachers in specific programs.

There also needs to be much more detailed study of localized contexts of Americanization as an *educational* and not just a political or cultural endeavor. This means a more systematic study of the educational processes that took place, which were used by specific educators in order to *attempt* to Americanize specific ethnic groups in specific localities. This also means a more detailed and focus look at teachers, teaching methods, curriculum, curriculum designers, educational materials and contexts, and funding. It also means looking into the institutional and

---

[123] Doug McAdam and W. Richard Scott, "Organizations and Movements" in *Social Movements and Organization Theory*. Gerald F. Davis, Doug McAdam, W. Richard Scott, and Mayer N. Zald, eds. (Cambridge: Cambridge University Press, 2005): 38.
[124] Kevin J. Dougherty, The Contradictory College: The Conflicting Origins, Impacts, and Futures of the Community College (1994; reprint, Albany, NY: State University of New York Press, 2001): 15-39, 105-6, 183-88, 239-42, 273-86.

organizational histories of normal schools and teacher training programs in order to see how teachers were prepared to become Americanizers. Educational and curricular purposes also need to be explored in relation to theories of ideology and, more particularly,
theories of nationalism as an ideology, cultural system, and site of cultural conflict.[125]

There also has been almost no work done on the larger effects or antecedents of the Americanization movement. Very few studies link the continental Americanization movement to U.S. imperialism. Robert A. Carlson's *The Quest for Conformity* touched on this connection, and several disconnected articles focusing on single colonized groups have discussed the issue of cultural and martial imperialism via Americanization in U.S. colonies like Puerto Rico, Hawaii, Guam, the Philippines, and the continental Americanization of Native Americans and African Americans. An important research question, which has not been full addressed by any historian, is the antecedent relationship between the 20th century Americanization movement and the 19th century Americanization efforts forced on Hawaiians, Philippinos, Native

---

[125] On ideology see several essays by Clifford Geertz, especially "Ethos, World View, and the Analysis of Sacred Symbols," "Ideology As a Cultural System," "The Politics of Meaning," and "Common Sense as a Cultural System" in *The Interpretation of Cultures: Selected Essays by Clifford Geertz* (New York: Basic Books, 1973) and *Local Knowledge: Further Essays in Interpretive Anthropology* (New York: Basic Books, 1983). See also: John B. Thompson *Studies in the Theory of Ideology* (Berkeley: University of California Press, 1984) and *Ideology and Modern Culture* (Stanford: Stanford University Press, 1990); J. M. Beach, *Studies in Ideology: Essays on Culture and Subjectivity* (Lanham: University Press of America, 2005): Part I and II. On social scientific theories and histories of nationalism see: Liah Greenfeld, *Nationalism: Five Roads to Modernity* (Cambridge: Harvard University Press, 1992); Guido Zernatto, "Nation: The History of a Word," *Review of Politics* 6 (1944): 351-66; Max Weber, *Wirtschaft und Gesellschaft* in *From Max Weber: Essays in Sociology*, H. H. Gerth and C. Wright Mills, eds. (1946; reprint, Oxford: Oxford University Press, 1958), 171-79; Louis Wirth, "Types of Nationalism," *The American Journal of Sociology* 41 (May 1936): 723-37; Hans Kohn, "The Nature of Nationalism," *The American Political Science Review* 33 (Dec 1939): 1001-21; Chong-Do Hah and Jeffrey Martin, "Toward a Synthesis of Conflict and Integration Theories of Nationalism," *World Politics* 27 (April 1975): 361-86; Isaiah Berlin, "Nationalism: Past Neglect and Present Power," *Against the Current: Essays in the History of Ideas*, in *The Proper Study of Mankind: An Anthology of Essays*, Henry Hardy and Roger Hausheer, eds. (1979; reprint, New York: Farrar, Straus and Giroux, 1997): 581-604; Benedict Anderson, *Imagined Communities: Reflections on the Origin and Spread of Nationalism* (1983; reprint, London: Verso, 1991); Eric Hobsbawm, *Nations and Nationalism since 1780: Programme, Myth, Reality* (1990; reprint, Cambridge: Cambridge University Press, 2000); Liah Greenfeld, "The Trouble with Social Science," *Critical Review* 17:1-2 (2005): 101-16.

Americans, and freed black slaves.[126]   Another important focus that has been almost completely ignored is the effect of the Americanization movement on the development of civic education in the public schools, and the development adult education in the newly formed community colleges.[127]   While there has been some treatment of the Americanization movement in the public schools by historians such as David Tyack and others (see footnotes 16 and 17), there has been no historical studies conducted to my knowledge, which have linked the Americanization movement to the widespread emergence of adult education or the origins of the community college.[128]

Understanding the emergence of American national identity, the expansion of the liberal state, the institutionalization of American identity in Americanization programs, and the growing geo-political power of the United States are all interconnected issues for 20th century historians and 21st century policy makers. David A. Hollinger used the older warning of David M. Potter as a branching off point to reevaluate the historian's usage of the nationalist paradigm.[129]   Hollinger warned, "Nations can easily turn historians into tools," but he added, "Nations are not the only formations that threaten to turn historians into tools. Nonnational and antinational movements and solidarities can do the same." Historians are always negotiating ideological, cultural, personal, or conceptual allegiances and they "select and deselect with every sentence." Besides,

---

[126] C. Kalani Beyer wrote an interesting article connecting Samuel Chapman Armstrong to both the Americanization of blacks and Hawaiians in "The Connection of Samuel Chapman Armstrong as Both Borrower and Architect of Education in Hawai'i," *History of Education Quarterly* 47:1 (Feb 2007): 2348. There is also an interesting article, which links social studies curriculum and civic training in the public schools to the Americanizing efforts done on African Americans at the manual training Hampton Institute in Virginia. This raises interesting questions about Americanization and social control in relation to oppressed, non-white minorities/non citizens and similar and/or differentiated treatment of citizen and/or "white" children in public schools. Michael Lybarger, "Origins of the Modern Social Studies: 1900 – 1916," *History of Education Quarterly* 23:4 (Winter 1983): 455-68.

[127] Emory S. Bogardus, *Essentials of Americanization* (Los Angeles: University of Southern California Press, 1919); Lawrence A. Cremin, *The Transformation of the School: Progressivism in American Education, 1876-1957* (New York: Vintage, 1961): 66-75; Morris Janowitz, *The Reconstruction of Patriotism: Education for Civic Consciousness* (Chicago: University of Chicago Press, 1983); Amy Gutmann, *Democratic Education* (Princeton: Princeton University Press, 1987): 104-107; Joel Westheimer, ed., *Pledging Allegiance: the Politics of Patriotism in America's Schools* (New York: Teachers College Press, 2007).

[128] Paul H. Sheats, "Adult Education for Victory and Peace," *Journal of Educational Sociology,* special issue on *The Foreign Born – Their Citizenship* 17:1 (Sep, 1943): 28-35; Caroline A. Whipple, "Adult Education and the Public Schools," *Journal of Educational Sociology* 19:1 (Sep, 1945): 20-26.

[129] David M. Potter, "The Historian's Use of Nationalism and Vice Versa," *The American Historical Review* 67 (July 1962): 924-50; David A. Hollinger, "The Historian's Use of the United States and Vice Versa," in *Rethinking American History in a Global Age*, Thomas Bender, ed. (Berkeley: University of California Press, 2002): 381-95.

Hollinger noted, "there is still substantial room for a national narrative that speaks to the American public, and that even has among its several purposes the critical maintenance of the United States considered as a political solidarity." Hollinger stated quite directly: "to study the nation is not necessarily to be an ideological nationalist." And he explained how there are many opportunities to describe power, inequality, and human agency within national narratives, and there is also room to deconstruct and historicize national identities as well: "How has the United States drawn and redrawn its social borders to accommodate, repel, or subjugate this or that group, in defiance of its egalitarian and individualistic self-image?" The study of Americanization, the early 20th century Americanization movement, and the multiple practices of Americanization programs by institutions and individuals comprise a complex ecology whereby issues of nationalism, internationalism, citizenship, patriotism, education, social control, exclusion, inequality, and social justice all come to the fore. This Gordian knot waits for future historians not to cut, but to unwind in order to trace the complicated contradictions of American nationalism and progressive politics which haunt this country still.

III

The Paradox of Progressivism:
A Definition of the Concept
and a Historiography of the Progressive
Era of United States History

The Paradoxical Concept of Progressivism

John R. Commons used the term "Progressive" in the 1890s as an idea foreshadowing a new social and political orientation that was challenging laissez-faire individualism, but he was not explicit about what the term meant. By 1897 Albion Small noticed a new reformist impulse in the U.S. and a rising "social movement," but was not sure if a few initial stirrings of reform would lead towards a programmatic platform that could create widespread social change.[130]   Daniel T. Rodgers has written that the word "progressive" was used by Woodrow Wilson in 1911, who prefaced its political meaning during the 1910 electoral campaigns by saying it was still a "new term." The rhetorical identification of a Progressive "movement" seemed to have arisen by around 1912 along with its ideological counterpart, "progressivism," which was used as a political orientation in opposition to the democratic, republican, and socialist parties. The prominence of these terms were due to the third-way "Progressive" Party in the presidential campaign of 1912, but these terms did not become associated with a widespread reformist identification until later in the decade.[131]

Benjamin Parke DeWitt published a polemic called *The Progressive Movement: A Non-partisan Comprehensive Discussion of Current Tendencies in American Politics* by 1915. He tried to explain the Progressive ideology and political platform in terms of a struggle between the oppressed "people" and the sinister political and economic "interests." By the time the so-called "Progressive movement" had largely come to an end after World War I, there was still no agreement on what exactly "Progressive" meant or what the movement was about. In 1924 *Nation* journalist William Hard held a contest to see if his readers could define "Progressivism." No consensus emerged.[132] During that same year, long time self-identified Progressive, Robert "Fighting Bob" La Follette, initiated a "new Progressive Party" (incorporating labor and socialists)

---

[130] John, R. Commons, "Progressive Individualism," *American Magazine of Civics,* 6 (June 1895), 561-74. Albion Small, "The Meaning of the Social Movement," *American Journal of Sociology,* 3 (Nov. 1897), 340-54.
[131] Daniel T. Rodgers, "In Search of Progressivism," *Reviews in American History* 10 (Dec 1982), 113-132. Rodgers' discussion of the origins of the term can be found in footnote 1.
[132] John D. Buenker, "Rejoinders," in *Progressivism* (Cambridge, MA: Schenkman Publishing Company, Inc, 1977), 113.

and was able to win 16% of the vote (the second largest third-party percentage of the 20th century, next only to the first Progressive Party of Roosevelt, which garnered over 4 million popular votes and 88 electoral votes). The year 1932 brought out an obituary for Progressivism in John Chamberlain's *Farewell to Reform: The Rise, Life and Decay of the Progressive Mind in America.*

During the 1950s and 60s the term "Progressivism" stood as the catch all concept of historians and political philosophers, which was used to define a broad age of liberal reform following agrarian uprisings ("Populism") and prefacing the New Deal. By the 1970's U.S. historians found the early 20th century social movement(s) ambiguous, inconsistent, paradoxical, contradictory, complex, and beyond the limited capacity of the term "Progressive."[133] Some called for the dismissal and burial of the term. But the idea survived and by 2003 Oxford University Press published yet another volume on the "Progressive Movement." We will look at selective portraits over the last 50 years within the historiography on the "Progressive Movement" to see how "Progressivism" has been defined in order to evaluate its usefulness as a concept for understanding U.S. reformist programs during the first decades of 20th century.

Richard Hofstadter was one of the first major historians of the "Progressive" period in U.S. history and also an early conceptualizer of "progressivism." He won the Pulitzer Prize in history for his treatment of the subject, *The Age of Reform* (1955). In this work he sought a "broader" definition of the term "progressive" and located its essence within the "impulse toward criticism and change" which was emblematic of middle-class programs for social and economic reform around the turn of the 20the century. He was careful to point out that both the larger term "Progressive" and the more specific "Progressive Movement" were "rather vague and not altogether cohesive or consistent" conceptions. He focused on the "ideas" of this vague and inconsistent movement, which was based on the notion of "self-reformation."[134]

Hofstadter described the United States economic, legal, and political system of the 19th century as "reliably conservative." He also noted that reactions against this conservative system of government during the 19th century were "popular," "democratic," and "progressive." Hofstadter labeled the period from 1890 to 1940 as an "age of reform," whereby, a "surge" of popular, democratic, and progressive reactions were sounded and corresponding social movements set forth. Hofstadter

---

[133] For a good, concise historiography of Progressivism up to the 1970s see William G. Anderson, "Progressivism: An Historiographical Essay," *The History Teacher* 6 (May, 1973), 427-52.

[134] Richard Hofstadter, *The Age of Reform, From Bryan to F.D.R.* (New York: Vintage Books, 1955), 5.

set the progressive period between two other periods of reform in U.S. history: 1) an earlier period of agrarian uprising, especially the "populist" movement, which had its origins in Jacksonian politics and reached it peak in the 1890s; 2) the progressive period, which properly congealed by 1900; and 3) the later initiative called the New Deal, originating in the 1930s, which was less programmatic, more pragmatic, and more Federally centered than previous reform periods. Hofstadter suggested that this long string of reformism had stalled by the 1950s (he was writing his book in mid decade), partly due to the social and political institutionalization of reform, which quite literally internalized the progressive-liberal ethos into the U.S. system of government and, thereby, argued Hofstadter, the progressive-liberal ethos as a political program became more conservative so as to preserve its central position within the socio-political arena.[135]

Hofstadter invoked several definitions and conceptions of "progressivism" and "progressives," but there were many common themes in his work. The Progressive Ethos was a broad "impulse" of "criticism and change" that became the "whole tone" of socio-political ferment after 1900. Its essence was an imprecise and nostalgic call for a "later-day Protestant revival" that preached "self-reformation," "economic individualism," "political democracy," "morality," and "civic purity." It was also a reactionary push against concentrated economic power, inequality, and corruption, while at the same time progressivism was a narrow-minded attempt to counter industrial inefficiency, urban social disorder, and immigration.

The Progressive actors were largely "genteel," "proper," and "respectable" middle class reformers with an "enthusiasm" for social and economic change. They had humanitarian "vision" and "courage," but they were not radicals and they preferred talk of "moral values" instead of initiating material improvement. Hofstadter also claimed that progressives were a group of "responsible" WASP "elites" who embarked on a "status revolution"[136] to regain "deference and power," which had been threatened by corporate capitalism, labor organizations, and ethnic political machines.

Hofstadter characterized the Progressive Movement as "rather vague," "not altogether cohesive or consistent," "mild and judicious," "moderate," "safe," and "constructive." This movement sought a "widespread" effort including "the greater part of society" for a "moderate" and "constructive" change in the social and political system.

---

[135] Ibid. 3, 10-14, 23-59, 133.
[136] A "status revolution" is perhaps Hofstadter's most contentious argument and it has been widely criticized by later historians of the period. Buenker, Burnham & Crunden (1977); Link & McCormick (1983); Chambers II (2000).

The movement seemed to prefer "exposure," "information," and "exhortation" to programmatic action and more equitable restructuring. Hofstadter noted the "radical" tenor of progressive criticisms, but he pointed out a "disparity between the boldness of their means and the tameness of their ends." He criticized the Progressive Movement as a "moral crusade" under the spell of an "evangelistic psychology" that often devolved into a "retrograde," "delusive," "comic," and sometimes "vicious" bit of political parody. Hofstadter made it clear that there was much about the Progressive Movement that could be considered illiberal and even unprogressive by its own standards.[137]

Another major historian of the Progressive period is Robert H. Wiebe whose *The Search for Order, 1877 – 1920* (1967) has been widely cited in the literature on the subject. Wiebe did not use the "Progressive" periodization and he did not refer to Progressives or Progressivism in his book, although it was mentioned in the "Introduction" by David Donald. The only time Wiebe used the term "Progressive" was in relation to the 3rd party during the 1912 presidential election, the "Progressive Party." Wiebe's book focused instead on what he terms "the new middle class." This group of people congealed into what could be called a "class" by the late 19th century and this "class" that Wiebe examines was conceptually similar to the "Progressives" that Hofstadter described. This new middle class was composed of educated and cultured professionals and specialists who were "clustered" in urban areas in the United States by the turn of the 20th century. These educated professionals had an optimistic "faith" in scientific and bureaucratic rationality and they tended to use this discursive method to focus on the country's "evils" with an "earnest desire to remake the world upon their private models." The primary goal of this new middle class was a desire for order, unity, efficiency, and cohesion in society, politics, industry, and urban development, both nationally and also internationally, in short they wanted a national – if not global – "frictionless bureaucracy." When order could not be achieved rationally, these professionals often resorted to "traditional techniques" to establish order, like force or exclusion: The new middle class would "draw a line around the good society and dismiss the remainder...separate the legitimate from the illegitimate." This new middle class used their scientific rationality to facilitate a new technocratic and managerial framework with which to gain power so as to "reorder" society, industry, and state according to what they considered universal, scientific principles of natural law.[138]

---

[137] Ibid. 5-6, 8-9, 11, 15-17, 19, 21, 135, 149, 152, 163-64, 182, 185-87, 196, 203, 206 211-12, 216, 288-301. These pages contain Hofstadter's major descriptions of Progressivism, Progressives, and the Progressive Movement. Hofstadter quotes "evangelistic psychology" from Fredric C. Howe's *The Confessions of a Reformer* (1925).
[138] Robert H. Wiebe, *The Search For Order, 1877 – 1920* (New York: Hill and Wang, 1967), 112-13, 128-29, 154-56, 161-68, 170, 174, 181, 198-99.

In 1968 James Weinstein wrote an important book and widely cited book on the influence of corporate capitalism on Progressive reform, *The Corporate Ideal in the Liberal State: 1900-1918.*[139] Weinstein demonstrated a "conscious and successful effort to guide and control the economic and social policies of federal, state, and municipal governments by various business groupings in their own long-range interest as they perceived it." Liberalism changed from its 19th century roots of individualism and laissez faire to an early 20th century "new liberalism" of corporate social responsibility and the rationalized expansion of the regulatory, "liberal" state. Many business leaders in the late 19th and early 20th century made a conscious decision to use liberal reform "as a means of securing the existing social [and economic] order." Liberal reforms were meant to incorporate various socialist and labor initiatives, while delegitimizing socialist and labor movements, and liberal reforms sought to stabilize, rationalize, and expand the apparatus of the state as a method business friendly of market regulation, which corporate interests could oversee or control. A member of the National Civic Federation and a utilities magnate, Samuel Insull, argued in 1909 that corporate leaders should "help shape the right kind of regulation" before "the wrong kind [was] forced upon him." At the Conference of Republicans of the State of New York in 1913, Elihu Root, also a member of the NCF, argued that the Republicans needed to "meet industrial and social demands of modern civilization, so far as they are reasonably consistent with our institutions." Paraphrasing Theodore Roosevelt, Weinstein argued that by the 1920s many corporation leaders began to see that "social reform was truly conservative." The rhetoric, legislation, oversight, and enforcement of worker collectives, trust regulation, workers compensation, reduction of the work day and work week, and wage increases could all be managed by corporate interests so as to safeguard the long term profits of corporate and monopoly capitalism from the more radical agitation of socialists and labor unions.[140] And as long as corporate leaders were willing to keep up a rhetorical front of corporate responsibility and regulation then political

---

[139] James Weinstein, *The Corporate Ideal in the Liberal State: 1900-1918* (Boston: Beacon Press, 1968).

[140] Weinstein argued that socialism was the "only serious ideological alternative to [the] politics of social responsibility" used by progressive and corporate coalitions, although he criticized the socialist tendency to place faith in the regulatory state without a full understanding of its corporate capitalist backers (117, 132).

leaders like Teddy Roosevelt, Wilson, Taft, and even Franklin Roosevelt were willing to conflate (using the rhetoric of "hearty cooperation") national with corporate and even monopoly interests. Even when truly concerned reformers like Frank P. Walsh tried to outline progressive industrial reforms, "the proposals were made mostly by men whose conscious purpose was to help the working man, while stabilizing and strengthening the corporate system," which lead to the "rise of a new corporate oligarchy."[141]

By 1970 "Progressivism" was being reexamined by historians. In "An Obituary for 'The Progressive Movement,'" Peter Filene called the whole conception of Progressivism and the Progressive Movement into question. He argued that what had been commonly called "The Progressive Movement" never actually happened. He said that there was never a monolithic and unified movement working towards a clear, let alone agreed upon, social and political program. The notion of a unified movement, Filene argued, was a "mirage." The concept of a "Progressive Movement" was a "dead end" because the data on reformers during the period from 1890 to 1930 "stubbornly spill[s] over the edges" of the concept of "Progressivism:" "The more historians learn, the farther they move from consensus." Filene argued that just because "many Americans in the early 20th century were 'reformers'" does not mean that "these Americans joined together in a 'reform movement.'" Filene argued, "The evidence points away from convenient synthesis and toward multiplicity" – social reform in the U.S. at the turn of the 20the century was "ambiguous, inconsistent, [and] moved by agents and forces more complex than a progressive movement."

And further, Filene argued, if there was a "progressive" ideology that united some reformers, it was "at best" "heterogeneous" and "lacked unanimity of purpose either on a programmatic or on a philosophic level." Filene even cited Michael Rogin's 1967 work *The Intellectuals and McCarthy: The Radical Specter* whose research questioned whether the Progressive Party could even be considered "progressive" based upon its diverse membership and contradictory platforms. Filene ended his article by focusing on the "diversity" of reformers during the period and the conflict and consensus between these diverse groups. He argued for a conception of "shifting coalitions around different issues" by which diverse reformers and reform groups practiced "political factionalism" and "ideological improvisation" in broad and contradictory efforts at reforming U.S. society, culture, and government.[142]

---

[141] Ibid., ix-xiii, 33, 58, 61, 143, 212, 252.
[142] Peter Filene, "An Obituary for 'The Progressive Movement,'" *American Quarterly* 22 (1970): 20-34;   John D. Buenker, John C. Burnham, and Robert M. Crunden, "Introduction," In *Progressivism* (Cambridge, MA: Schenkman Publishing Company, Inc., 1977), iv-viii.

In response to Filene's charge, three respected and widely published scholars in the area of early 20th century U.S. history published *Progressivism* (1977). In this book John C. Burnham, John D. Buenker, and Robert M. Crunden each drafted a statement and a rejoinder to discuss the usefulness and accuracy of "Progressivism" as a tool for understanding early 20th century political and social reform in the U.S.[143]

In the first essay John C. Burnham argued that Filene's "obituary" was "premature" because Filene along with other scholars had focused too much on particular aspects of the diverse political and local history of the period, which "ended up refining progressivism out of existence." Burnham argued that "Progressivism" needed to be re-evaluated and he suggested two new ways to conceptualize the term: 1) the "coalescing" of a number of reformist streams that "reinforced" each other, "cumulating" into "what contemporaries recognized as progressivism;" and 2) specific socio-political "changes" that actually occurred around the turn of the 20th century.[144]

Burnham invoked Clyde Griffen's concept of a "progressive ethos," which was defined as an "an idealism marked by the 'juxtaposition of a practical piece-meal approach to reform with a religious or quasi-religious vision of democracy.'"[145] Burnham argued that this "progressive ethos," an optimistic and scientific "moral fervor" to change the world, sparked a "progressive movement" around 1907-08 when journalistic criticism gave way to direct action and, thereby, inspired a "confluence of specific reform streams." These reform streams were primarily based within non-governmental voluntary organizations because progressives were "ambivalent" if not "mistrustful" of government action.[146] Burnham argues that while "concrete achievements" outside of formal organizational efforts (membership lists, meetings, organizational literature) are "hard to demonstrate," the membership numbers and sheer diversity of organizations was testament to the "awesome demonstration of the power of determined private

---

[143] John D. Buenker, John C. Burnham, and Robert M. Crunden, *Progressivism* (Cambridge, MA: Schenkman Publishing Company, Inc., 1977).

[144] John C. Burnham, "Essay," in *Progressivism* (Cambridge, MA: Schenkman Publishing Company, Inc, 1977), 3-29.

[145] Burnham is quoting Clyde Griffen, "The Progressive Ethos," in *The Development of an American Culture*, eds. Stanley Coben and Lorman Ratner (Englewood Cliffs, N.J., 1970): 120-149.

[146] Burnham argued against claims linking progressivism to welfare statism: "Equating the extension of governmental power for social justice purposes, or what came to be called welfare statism, to the spirit of progressivism is therefore an error. It is true that many Americans admired German cameralism and socialism. And many Americans did come to think that the neutral state would have to intervene more actively to maintain traditional liberty and freedom in society and so become a service state. But to portray the attitudes of progressives toward political activity and power as anything beyond ambivalence is to distort the movement beyond recognition" (15).

citizens." Progressivism was also a "practical evangelism" based on professionalism, efficiency, expertise, and science, which lead to an "ideal of unselfish service and efficiency," which in turn manifested itself in programs providing care, service, and protection. These aid programs, carried out primarily by voluntary organizations, sought to reform behavior and change people – socially, politically, culturally, morally, hygienically, and linguistically. Often reform organizations used education and persuasion to bring about this change, but coercion was not out of the question, especially when progressives thought reform was necessarily in the best interests of the recipient.

Robert M. Crunden's "Essay"[147] drew on the work of Eric Erikson[148] and argued that "progressivism" was a "frame of mind" or "frame of reference" composed of basic "moral and emotional attitudes" that many of the "leaders" of the reform period shared. Crunden believed that Progressivism was not "specifically political or social, but rather cultural" to which he added, "progressivism was essentially religious" – a "form of displaced Protestantism:" Progressivism was the "spirit" and the "motivation" that inspired reformers. Crunden defined a Progressive as "a person of strongly religious upbringing who displaced the moral concerns of his youth onto the very real social, industrial, political and aesthetic problems of his maturity, and who attempted to solve these public and personal problems within a Protestant, moral frame of reference." Crunden held up Jane Addams and John Dewey as "psychological paradigms of the progressive experience." Crunden also quotes Frederic C. Howe, a self-described reformer, who earlier wrote about the Progressive's "evangelistic psychology:

---

[147] Robert M. Crunden, "Essay," in *Progressivism* (Cambridge, MA: Schenkman Publishing Company, Inc, 1977), 71-103.
[148] Crunden summarized Erikson's theory in this way: "Erikson has demonstrated suggestively how crises in childhood and youth can combine especially with religious milieus to produce effective political movements, and to create moral frames of reference in which certain values and reactions seem to be taken for granted. He has also placed his considerable prestige behind the contention that great leaders articulate and find ways of resolving the important psychological conflicts in the culture of their time" (72). Crunden draws from Erikson, *Childhood and Society* (New York, 1950, 1963); *Young Man Luther* (New York, 1958); *Ghandi's Truth* (New York, 1969). See also Robert M. Crunden, "Freud, Erikson and the Historian: A Bibliographical Survey," *Canadian Review of American Studies* vol. 4, no. 1 (Spring, 1973): 48-64.

I was conformed to my generation and made to share its moral standards and ideals…early assumptions as to virtue and vice, goodness and evil remained in my mind long after I had tried to discard them. This is, I think, the most characteristic influence of my generation. It explains the nature of our reforms, the regulatory legislation in morals and economics, our belief in men rather than in institutions and our messages to other peoples…all a part of that evangelistic psychology that makes America what she is.[149]

While Crunden argued that Progressives were primarily motivated by religious and psychological concerns, he did not discount or deny that other factors, like economical or political motivations, also played a part. Crunden argued that many historians mistake economic and political motivations as the whole story. Crunden argued that the Progressive Movement can best be understood in relation to the "psychological needs of the reformer."

Crunden's essay in *Progressivism* was expanded several years later into a book, *Ministers of Reform: The Progressives' Achievement in American Civilization, 1889 – 1920* (1982). In this work Crunden again argued that Progressivism was an "ethos," a "dominant national mood," and a "system of values," which grew out of the individual psychological needs of a culturally transitioning and professionalizing middle class. He argued that Progressives shared no single political or social platform nor were they members of a single reform movement. Progressives shared "moral values" and a commitment to the "spiritual reformation" of American democracy, and while the Progressive ethos often seemed "amorphous, inchoate, and difficult to define," it was bounded by a Protestant and democratic discourse and infused by a moral fervor to reform all facets of U.S. society. Crunden denied that there was a "progressive era," and instead focused on three generations of U.S. reformism: liberal precursors of Progressivism [reformers born before 1854], 1st generation Progressives [reformers born between 1854 – 1874], and 2nd generation Progressives [reformers born between 1874 – 1894]. Crunden's book makes several historical character sketches of individual Progressives, like Jane Addams, John Dewey, George Herbert Mead, and George Herron, in order to describe how a "progressive ethos" infused these individuals' specific reformist impulse.[150]

---

[149] Fredric C. Howe, *The Confessions of A Reformer* (1925; reprint, Chicago, 1967), 12-17. Crunden, "Essay," *Progressivism*, 98-99.
[150] Robert M. Crunden, *Ministers of Reform: The Progressives' Achievement in American Civilization, 1889 – 1920* (1982; reprint, Urbana: University of Illinois Press, 1984), ix-x, 39-40, 64-68,164, 274-277.

John D. Buenker's "Essay" in *Progressivism*[151] marked a growing divergence on the subject. He stood in agreement with Filene's "shifting coalitions" theory and against the "ethos" theory of scholars like Burnham and Crunden. Buenker argued that since "Progressivism" had been defined so many ways it had lost clear meaning except in relation to a specific political party and, thus, Buenker claimed, "as a description of either an ideology or a political program, I find it worthless and misleading." Buenker argued that trying to define Progressivism as a "common set of values" was disingenuous because it either gets defined too broadly (and thus just about every middle class person at the turn of the century could be described as "Progressive") or it gets defined too narrowly (and thus becomes "ambiguous" and "contradictory" in relation to specific individuals).

Buenker argued that there were many Progressive populations and programs and each had a different set of values. Thus he believed that Filene's "shifting coalitions" conception seemed the most appropriate theory with which to describe the various early 20th century reform movement(s). Buenker argued that the idea of shifting coalitions was a more "comprehensive explanation" because it can take into account diverse reform movements composed of diverse people with diverse motives who may have on certain occasions accommodated or cooperated on specific reform issues: "the politics of compromise, conciliation, and coalition," Buenker noted, "have been the hallmark of the American system from the beginning." A focus on shifting coalitions put primary emphasis on the political arena as the plane where compromise, conciliation, and coalition took place.[152] But he also noted that individual reformers had complex identities and conflicting social relationships, which in turn further fractured any coherent notion
of personal "ethos" that a historian might construct. Buenker demanded a complex reckoning of the specific social, cultural and political relationships and identities of individual reformers both prior to and during public reform debates and policy coalitions.[153]

---

[151] John D. Buenker, "Essay," in *Progressivism* (Cambridge, MA: Schenkman Publishing Company, Inc, 1977), 31-69.
[152] Buenker wrote: "In a larger sense, Americans turned to politics because it was the only forum the nation possessed for ameliorating the conditions wrought by industrialization, immigration, and urbanization and for accommodating the competing demands of various economic, ethnic, and geographic groups...In a highly competitive society there was not a real sense of community to sustain concern for the less fortunate. For better or worse, only politics provided an arena where conflicting groups could face each other under established ground rules and attempt to resolve their differences. The political system, alone of America's institutions, was based upon the existence of pluralism and diversity; it was constructed by compromise and specially designed to provide a means of accommodating conflicting interests" (46-47).
[153] Ibid., 31-40, 43, 56, 59 63.

Daniel T. Rogers offered a look at the concept of "progressivism" in 1982.[154] He noted that the term went from "one of the central organizing principles of American history" to a "corpse that would not lie down." The debate of the meaning of progressivism was "acute and troubling." He described the literature on the subject after 1970 as moving away from the ethos of Progressivism and actors in a Progressive movement to its "context" – the "structures of politics, power, and ideas within which the era's welter of tongues and efforts and 'reforms' took place." The "fundamental fact" researchers of the 1970s focused on was the "explosion of scores of aggressive, politically active pressure groups" in an era of "shifting, ideologically fluid, issue-focused coalitions, all competing for the reshaping of American society" of which the Progressives were only one group. Actually, Rogers argued, the group of reformers called the "Progressives" were really many distinct individuals and associations that "shared no common party or organization," had "deep disagreements," but from time to time shared ideas and rhetorical strategies.[155] Progressive politics, like other forms of politics in the era, were "coalition politics, prone to internal fissures." And this was perhaps one of the distinctive features of the era, the "rise of modern, weak-party, issue-focused politics." The other distinctive feature was the "revolution" in "social organization:" "the eclipse of the local, informal group" and its "replacement by vastly bigger, bureaucratically structured formal organizations," most importantly the business corporation and the regulatory state. Rogers spent some time reviewing the literature of New Left historians like Gabriel Kolko and James Weinstein whose research described the "new corporate phase of capitalism," which allowed the corporation to become the "dominant" economic force of the 20th century.

In 1983 Arthur S. Link and Richard L. McCormick published a short but detailed historiographical summary of the literature on Progressivism up to 1980. Link and McCormick organized the previous scholarly literature into six schools of analysis:

1)   a conflict between "ordinary" and wealthy Americans

---

[154] Daniel T. Rodgers, "In Search of Progressivism," *Reviews in American History* 10 (Dec 1982), 113-132.

[155] Rogers argued that Progressives did not "share a common creed or a string of common values," but instead shared a "cluster of ideas" and "three distinct social languages." These languages were a "rhetoric of antimonopolism," "an emphasis on social bonds and the social nature of human beings," and "the language of social efficiency." Rodgers said the Progressives were great "users" of ideas as a "set of tools" with which they made "progressive social thought distinct and volatile" as they brought together all three of the reformist languages together into a powerful and "dynamic" "constellation" "from which they drew their energies and their sense of social ills, and within which they found their solutions" (122-27).

2)	the continuation of a long tradition of agrarian protest
3)	an urban, WASP, professional, middle-class movement trying to organize society, thereby, remedying industrialization, urbanization, and immigration
4)	an urban, WASP, professional, middle-class movement on an intolerant moral crusade to remake America inspired mostly by their own personal problems
5)	reformers from the "wealthiest" groups of society out to address social ills
6)	diverse reform groups with divergent missions who often formed "shifting coalitions" to address and combat particular issues

For all six schools, Link and McCormick warned, historians have not often separated "purposes, rationale, and results" in their research. These are three very different yet mutually informative categories of analysis. The authors pointed out how many historical studies of the period have exaggerated a single category of analysis to the exclusion of others.

Despite all the diversity on the subject, Link and McCormick did offer their own summation of "Progressivism." They noted there was "no unified movement," but many "diverse" and "convulsive reform movements" with many diverse and contradictory goals that came through the U.S. between the 1890s and 1917. These reform movements were typically led by "crusading" middle- and upper-class, native-born, professional Americans who sought in one way or another to address and ameliorate specific social ills, especially those social problems resulting from urbanization and industrialization. The typical Progressive reform pattern began with investigation of a problem, which led to organizing a response, which in turn led to educating the citizenry, and often ended with the pinnacle of Progressive reform – legislation: Reformers "assumed that passing a law was equivalent to solving a problem and that government officials could be entrusted to enforce the measure in a progressive spirit." And while different reform movements and leaders articulated distinctive discourses of social justice, they were all usually "simplistic, traditional, moralistic" and programmatically warranted some kind of narrowly defined social control. Specifically, the authors pointed out an often neglected aspect of Progressivism: "coercive" Progressives.

Coercive Progressive programs sought to impose social control and they took various forms, like the White Jim Crow movement in the South, Americanization programs, and moral reforms such as temperance and prohibition. While they made many references within the literature to the problematic usage of "Progressive," Link and McCormick argued in passing, "it might be better to avoid the terms progressive and progressivism altogether, but they are too deeply embedded in the language of contemporaries and historians to be ignored."[156]

In 1987 Nell Irvin Painter published her award winning treatment of the Progressive Era, *Standing at Armageddon: The United States, 1877 – 1919.*[157] She analyzed the politics of the era via a "hybrid political-labor history" framework. This schema allowed her to focus on the "conflict between various groups, classes, and competing ideals," which morphed into a pitched battle between "partisans of democracy" and "protectors of hierarchy" – "the struggle over the distribution of wealth and power." This great political conflict and struggle caused enormous amounts of "fear...plain, stark fear" in the hearts and minds of the middle- and upper-class. Painter argued that this fear "lay at the core" of many "progressive reforms." The table below displays the large gap between the very rich (0.01%), the rich (11%), and the rest of the country (88%). The great extremes of wealth caused by capitalism and industrialization became a point of concern for the great majority who owned less than 15% of the national wealth.

Distribution of Wealth and Income in U.S.A. (1890)

Class Status	% of U.S. Pop.	% of U.S. Wealth	# of Families	Mean $ per Family
Rich	0.01%	50.8%	125,000	$264,000
Upper Middle	11%	35.4%	1,375,000	$16,000
Middle	44%	13%	5,500,000	$1,500
Poor	44%	1.2%	5,500,000	$150(poverty $544)

---

[156] Arthur S. Link and Richard L. McCormick, *Progressivism* (Wheeling, IL: Harlan Davidson, Inc., 1983), 1-10, 21-22, 72, 79, 84, 96-104.
[157] Nell Irvin Painter, *Standing at Armageddon: The United States, 1877 – 1919* (New York: W. W. Norton & Company, 1987).

Painter stressed that while income does provide the "single clearest indicator of class standing," the notion of class needed to be seen as a complex, "fluid" and ever changing classification, whereby there was no single "middle class," but rather "middle classes" (and also "many ethnicities and races"). Those elite classes with the most at stake and thereby the most influence liked to put forth ideological arguments for the "identity of interest." This belief conceptualized society as a smoothly functioning organism wherein the interests of the great capitalists and property owners were supposedly the best interests of all in society and in harmony with "laws of God or Science." Reformers acting as "democratizers" put forth a counter-conception of society. Seeing their own middle-class or working-class interests at odds with those of capitalists and industrialists, democratizers saw society torn by a "conflict of interests." Reformers often, but not always, tried to point out the interests of the "disadvantaged" within the social system and thereby argue for "the ideal of equity" and democracy, in order to confront the dangerous extremes of wealth and privilege. But lurking at the periphery of all calls for reform was the specter of working class unrest, which from time to time would boil into a froth and cause conflicts of interest to turn into real (and often violent) social and political struggles for power. The so called "Progressive Era" was marked by a widespread call for reform and social change, however, as Painter pointed out, "the broadening consensus that change was necessary did not include agreement on the direction or extent of these changes."[158]

Perhaps the most powerful voice of reform came from educated and elite men who wanted a more "clean, efficient government" operated by a rationalized bureaucratic machinery and run by an advanced cadre of elite professionals. Painter argued that reform initiatives during the period were often very "ambiguous" and rarely a "straightforward story of altruism" because "nativism, racism, and sexism" pervaded both the reformist impulses and the reformist programs of these educated elites. By the early 20th century many middle class and agrarian reformers, including the so-classed Progressives (like the Progressive Party's presidential candidate, Teddy Roosevelt), saw the United Stats as standing on the threshold of "Armageddon" with the evils of plutocratic industrial power on one side and the evils of the violent mob on the other. Progressives under the banners of "New Nationalism" or "New Freedom" called for the regulation of society and the economy by an empowered and enlightened federal government which would act as a disinterested arbitrator between conflicting political factions, like labor and capital (of course more radical voices pointed out the impossibility of a disinterested federal government as federal policy was often in the hands of industrial capitalists and their appointed voices in the Congress). Teddy Roosevelt

---

[158] Ibid., xii-xiii, xix, xxiv, xl, xliii, 279-80.

succinctly summarized the ideals of these Progressive reformers: "the object of the government is the welfare of the people. The material progress and prosperity of a nation are desirable chiefly so far as they lead to the moral and material welfare of all good citizens."[159]

The most frightening voice of reform came from the laboring classes and political radicals who often spoke in the name of working class interests. Often disposed and exploited, lacking any real propertied interest in the social order, workers expressed their frustration through "strikes, boycotts, and cooperative enterprises" in order to pool their collective strength as a means to gain bargaining leverage with their industrial masters. It was not until the late 19th century that workers and radicals, especially socialists, began turning to the political process and electoral politics as a way of "influencing" the U.S. economy and factory workplaces. Labor and Populist leaders began to see that "they would have to take a hand in shaping the laws that governed them," which meant lobbying the state and federal governments "to seize the powers to regulate" the industrial economy on the "behalf" of working class interests. Women and ethnic minorities also tried to use the political process in order to highlight their marginal status and seek redress through political rights, but these efforts were largely unsuccessful during the "Progressive Era," with the exception of white women who were able to gain suffrage by the end of WWI.[160]

Painter also talked at length about race and racism in the U.S. She discussed the racialized U.S. foreign policy and imperialist interventionist projects of the period. Formally mapped out in 1885 at the Berlin Conference, the world had been divided by white Europeans, and also by the turn of the century Japan. By 1900 Europeans ruled over 1/5 of the world's land and 1/10 of the world's human population. Each dominant European nation assigned itself "national spheres of interest" over which each nation, through soft and hard exercises of colonial mastery, exploited favorable terms of trade and natural resource extraction. The U.S. via a revitalized Monroe Doctrine asserted control over the Americas and the Caribbean with expansive moves across the Pacific and into China. With some envy for the preeminent stature of Great Britain, Painter argued that an "Anglo-American identity of interest" coupled with an "Anglo-Saxon chauvinism" congealed in the later 19th century as the English-speaking countries united under the racialized banner of "the natural superiority of Anglo-Saxons." After the

---

[159] Ibid., xxviii, 8, 136, 258, 268.
[160] Ibid., 70-71, 231-52.

conquest of the Philippines president McKinley wrapped U.S. foreign policy in this doctrine of "the white man's burden." He stated that the Filipinos could not be left to themselves because "they were unfit for self-government" and, thus, the Americans had a duty "to take them all, and to educate the Filipinos, and uplift and civilize and Christianize them, and by God's grace do the very best we could by them." Indiana Senator Albert J. Beveridge believed that the "American Republic" was destined, through the will of God and the dictates of the "highest law" of "race," to be "the most masterful race in history." Painter explained: "Imperialism was elemental, racial, predestined, for God had prepared the English-speaking people, master organizers, for governing what Beveridge called 'save and senile people.'" Even anti-imperialists, who argued against the trappings of empire for many reasons, often framed their critiques of foreign intervention with the same racist assumptions, and focused more on the implications of empire for poor whites in America. Many Southerners actually felt vindicated by Imperial policies, although skeptical about ruling over more non-white people. Benjamin Tillman argued to his fellows in Congress that "We of the South" had already "borne this white man's burden of a colored race in our midst." In 1883 the Supreme Court had already invalidated the Civil Rights Act of 1875 and by the 1890s there was widespread acceptance of Jim Crow segregation and disenfranchisement laws. The color line became an increasingly important national preoccupation by the early 20th century as the U.S. became defined more and more as a white man's nation. Thus self-proclaimed "progressives" never touched the white supremacy of the South and *de facto* "racial hierarchy" of the country as a whole.[161]

Another article by John D. Buenker published in 1988 argued for the existence of "two full-blown political cultures," which influenced and defined the socio-political and cultural identifications of Americans during the turn of the 20th century.[162] Despite the "complexity and diversity of motives, goals, methods, and results" of socio-political and cultural struggle during this period, Buenker argued for two distinctive and primary "competing political cultures." These two political cultures were especially important in defining the relationship between the individual and society, and they set up distinctive battle lines within the "arena of structural reform:" 1) the "new politics" of a "modernizing" ideology of "atomistic aggregation of sovereign individuals," which was associated with the "reformer-individualist-Anglo-Saxon complex," and 2) the "old politics" of an "ethnic identification" of "organic networks,"

---

[161] Ibid., Ch 5 & 7.
[162] John D. Buenker, "Sovereign Individuals and Organic Networks: Political Cultures in Conflict During the Progressive Era," *American Quarterly* 40 (Jun, 1988), 187-204.

which was aligned with the "boss-immigrant-machine complex." Buenker argued that these two world views shaped the context out of which individuals defined their socio-political-cultural identities and allegiances, but they should not be seen as some oversimplified dualism: "The choice made by individuals was not a dichotomous one between the sovereign individualist or organic network world views. Rather, the two views functioned as antipodes on a continuum or as the rows and columns of a matrix on which each person found his or her own identity out of a bewildering variety of permutations that changed over the life cycle." The Progressive coalition would have been associated with the "new politics" and part of their mission, under the terms Buenker introduced in this essay, was to confront and defeat the "old politics" for control over the socio-political-cultural reform that would govern the new century.

In 1999 Alan Dawley published a major work on the broad period of reform infusing the early 20th century: *Struggles for Justice: Social Responsibility and the Liberal State.* The central question of his book (and the broad period of reform under study) was not about Progressivism but about "how could the existing form of the state, designed generations earlier for an agrarian-commercial society, withstand the brawling conflicts and relentless evolution of an urban-industrial way of life?" Dawley argued that the "crux of American history" around the turn of the 20th century was the "reckoning between a dynamic society and the existing liberal state." Progressivism was only a small, but important part of this much larger and very global issue.

His book broke down the reckoning of state and society into three stages. The first stage was "imbalance" and he located this stage between the 1890s and 1913. During this period U.S. society was "on a collision course" with its political system based on laissez-faire liberalism and the inequality it bred. Liberty and political right were "reserved" for wealthy, white men and as other groups struggled for socio-political inclusion, the "polarities of class and culture intensified" and "struggles broke out" across the nation. Many reform initiatives reacted to this conflict so as to resolve it, but different reformers often fostered conflicting visions, which only furthered the melee. And behind it all, Dawley argued, was a "contradiction between the needs of society and the existing political system." The next stage, from 1914 to 1924, was a time of "confronting issues" by the state resulting in an increase in state intervention and regulation, whereby, the "governing system" of "state embedded in society" began to change in dialectical relation to social struggles. The last stage from 1925 to 1938 marked a "resolution" of state intervention to "restore balance" to the governing system. The New Deal was the primary institutional impetus of this resolution, but Dawley was quite clear in arguing that this new policy program focused on "neither liberty nor equality, but security."

At the center of Dawley's book was the "problem of hegemony:" "how was society held together (consensus) against its own inner contradictions (conflict)?" One of the central arguments he made towards explaining the successful change within the governing system was the power and strategy of elites "to regain their legitimacy by reforming the system." He links progressivism to "managerial liberalism" and "social liberalism" as viable forms of state interventionism that could accommodate reformist demands for social change while legitimizing elite management of the social and political transformations. As a solidly liberal and yet quasi-socialist ideology, Progressivism was able to "contain" socialism and thus middle-class and elite interests were able to steer reformist initiatives in more conservative and capitalist directions that did not significantly challenge the institutional structure of liberal society. Dawley argued that it was "inevitable" that "state structures and ruling values would change" – "the only questions were how, and in whose interests?" In terms of early 20th century reform initiatives and state interventionism, Dawley wrote, "Americans were dragged kicking and screaming toward social responsibility."[163] Thus Progressivism, in Dawley's conception, was a response to challenge the excesses and instability of the elite managed liberal state while containing the more threatening challenges and disorder of lower class unrest.

John Whiteclay Chambers II first published *The Tyranny of Change: American in the Progressive Era, 1890 – 1920* in 1992. He noted that many historians have written about the "Progressive Era," but they have not been clear about "the nature of either progressivism or the era."[164] Despite this confusion, he argued the concepts of a "progressive impulse or ethos" and a "Progressive Era" continued to be "relevant." He noted that while Progressivism was not a united movement, it was still "the most pervasive political reform effort since the pre-Civil War period." He called Progressivism a "controversial and complex," "multifaceted," "moderate" reform movement that "affected nearly every aspect of American life." He also acknowledged the shifting coalitions theory by stating how a "hodgepodge of coalitions" often "contradicted each other" while working for "diverse" social change. However, while he denied Progressives a "common creed or a system of

---

[163] Alan Dawley, *Struggles for Justice: Social Responsibility and the Liberal State* (Cambridge: Belknap Press of Harvard University Press, 1991), 1-13, 30-31, 62, 71-73, 105, 128-38, 163-65, 370, 394.
[164] Chambers noted in his bibliography that he was not able to read Dawley's *Struggles for Justice* in researching the first edition of his book. I would argue that Dawley has presented one of the clearest and most comprehensive treatments of the era and the subject of Progressivism to date.

values," he also described what he believed to be some common "clusters of ideas" and "social languages," like democratic ideals, rhetorical appeals to move people, a "politics of opposition." Whiteclay argued that Progressives were not often original thinkers, but there were powerful "users" of ideas in the effort to initiate social change.

Chambers devoted a whole chapter to the "Progressive Impulse" in which he defined "Progressivism" as a "nationwide movement" composed of a "number of major efforts to reform society through the power of private groups and public agencies." Leaders and participants of *some* of these reform efforts called themselves "Progressives," and hence the label often given for the whole period, but there were many radical and conservative reformers as well. Chambers noted, Progressives "battled conservatives, radicals, other reformers, and often each other." Acknowledging the multiplicity of ideological reform groups was a marked change in direction as most historians up to this point had tended to focus mostly on those particular individuals and groups who claimed the "Progressive" mantle.

Chambers noted that recent scholarship in the 1990s had emphasized the socio-political contexts of reform ("the environment of politics, power, ideas, and values"), and

also the role of the state, specifically the relationships between different "political structures" and particular social groups. Perhaps the most notable new direction in the historiography of the period had been Chambers' use of the term "the new interventionists" to describe the whole, broad reform movement of the period, which included Progressives, but also included the many other ideological reform groups of the period   The new interventionists used voluntary associations and sometimes the state to challenge 19th century lassie faire individualism and free-market capitalism and this challenge took many forms: Progressives, moderates, conservatives, traditionalists, and radical activists like socialists, communists, and anarchists. The new interventionists, Chambers claimed, left a "divided legacy." They seemed to have been more successful "at arousing indignation and protest than at maintaining effective government and substantially ameliorating urban problems." They also over-relied on strong leadership and monolithic reform visions that often led to "the tyranny of change," whereby, the general public supported or elected strong leaders but had very little impact on public planning or policy.[165]

William Deverell argued that by 1994 the concepts of "progressivism" and "progressive" carried "diverse and heavy burdens of meaning," which made many scholars believe that these terms had "outlived their usefulness as meaningful expressions by which to explain" the past: these concepts had lost, in the words of Martin Sklar, their "interpretive precision."[166] But Deverell argued that scholars must not loose sight of the fact that "individuals, parties, and groups used the terms *progressive* and *progressivism* to define themselves, their work, and their outlook as the new century arrived." He stressed that there was an "historical context" within which these terms were "borrowed, taken, utilized, even invented" and scholars and historians would do well to admit that these terms "once meant something" before these terms become jettisoned for more precise conceptualizations. Deverell noted that while progressivism had become "an embattled word, an embattled concept," real derivatives from the "progressive phenomenon" were still visible in the current socio-political climate and discourse: "Progressivism is alive and well four score years after its birth."

---

[165] John Whiteclay Chambers II, *The Tyranny of Change: American in the Progressive Era, 1890 – 1920* (1992; reprint, New Brunswick, NJ: Rutgers University Press, 2000), xi-xiii, 132-47, 150-51, 157, 169-71. Chambers summed up nicely the "meaning of the Progressive Era:" "In the Progressive Era, large numbers of Americans concluded that the problems accompanying industrialization meant that they could no longer rely solely on Providence or evolution for automatic progress. They lost their faith in the long-held utilitarian concept of a natural harmony of self-interests and in the functioning of a self-regulating society...With optimism and the sense of power that came from developments in science, technology, and organizational theory, the new interventionists decided that it was necessary to modify the concept of unrestricted individualism and the marketplace. They thought that intervention and intelligent direction could ensure continued growth and progress that would be consistent with the ideal of an efficient and liberal democratic society...Interventionists created new mechanisms for dealing with the problems caused by blind social forces or powerful, self-interested individuals or groups...interventionists employed organization and intervention as tools for achieving their goals and imposing conscious direction on society...The dominant development of the era was the emergence of an interventionist mood on a national scale. The need for some kind of purposeful, collective intervention...the organization of economic and social power. The local, informal group so characteristic of small-town and agrarian society was superseded as the basic framework of American life by immensely larger, hierarchically structured formal organizations...the organizational or bureaucratic revolution....Although people at all levels of society sought to influence the forces affecting their lives, particularly in the immediate environment in which they lived, the poor and the unorganized had little or no influence in the national political system" (275-82).
[166] William Deverell, "The Varieties of Progressive Experience," *California Progressivism Revisited*, ed. William Deverell and Tom Sitton (Berkeley: University of California Press, 1994): 1-11.

Gary Gerstle's "The Protean Character of American Liberalism" (1994) discussed the changing ethos of American liberalism from the turn of the twentieth century to the New Deal.[167] Gerstle argued, it is "unwise to treat the liberal community as a stable political entity or to presume that the criteria for identifying liberals in one period can be applied to another. Any effort to define the liberal community must be firmly located in time and space." Gerstle noted that the "liberal tradition" had three "foundational principles" (emancipation, rationality, and progress), but overall liberalism had a marked "malleability" that made for variant socio-political programs and ideologies.

Classical liberalism revolved around free markets, limited statism, and bourgeois morality, which often defended corporate capitalism, segregation and disenfranchisement. By the end of the 19th century liberalism displayed a reformist edge and it organized "rational interventions in society and culture," often by turning "to the state as an institutional medium capable of reconstructing society and of educating citizens." Progressivism was a three pronged liberal reaction to (a) socialism and labor radicalism, (b) the "extraordinary concentration of power and wealth," and (c) a diverse influx of immigrating ethnic groups. Progressives wanted to find ways to promote and protect "freedom of trade and individual liberty" by way of state regulation and welfare, and by way of "guild socialism." They also wanted to engage in "cultural reconstruction" because liberals believed in the importance of individual moral character as the foundation of civic virtue. When dealing with foreigners this "reconstruction" took the form of "Americanization" in order to "culturally and morally transform...aliens into citizens." But Progressives were a diverse bunch ("left-leaning Progressives" ranging from socialists to left leaning pluralists, and "rightward-leaning Progressives" from Americanizers to hard core nationalists preaching "100 percent Americanism") and because of these conflicts of purposes and methods they "had difficulty fashioning a cultural politics to which they could all adhere," which eventually lead to a loss of "coherence as a political movement."

During World War I and the Red Scare Progressives felt themselves and their ideological convictions to be "impotent in the face of a reactionary nationalism." Liberals largely "give up the fight to create a new culture and new nationalism," and began to ignore the "irrational" realm of culture to focus instead on the more rational and therefore changeable realm of economics and political economy. This lead to a widespread "exclusion of ethnicity and race" from liberal social scientific analysis, which lead to a "more narrowly conceived" liberal program of

---

[167] Gary Gerstle, "The Protean Character of American Liberalism," *The American Historical Review* 99:4 (Oct 1994): 1043-1073.

economic recovery during the New Deal years. It took the rise of Hitler and the Nazi party to bring back liberal discussions of "racial and ethnic discrimination." After World War II liberals once again "reconstituted" their political focus and began to define "issues of ethnicity and race as appropriate targets of rational social action," while treating "class politics as an expression of irrationality" and therefore beyond the scope of liberal intervention.

In 1997 Eric Foner edited a volume for the American Historical Association that offered a look at the "new" American history written over the last 20 years. Within this volume Richard L. McCormick talked about Progressivism and other reform impulses in "Public Life in Industrial America, 1877 – 1917."[168] In this essay McCormick claimed that the central issue of this period was industrialization and modernization, and how individuals and groups addressed the unsettling consequences of these two developments. There is no "coherent synthesis," McCormick argued, for describing the "complex" social, political and cultural reactions to industrialization and modernization. There were "many organized endeavors" that produced many "unexpected results." But McCormick did argue for some common themes:

> Most people confronted variations on a common problem: the defense of their families and communities against outside forces emanating from industrial growth and the increasing heterogeneity of the population. Americans faced that problem, moreover, within a common environment: a rapidly expanding economy that was causing massive dislocations, frequent depressions, and widespread unemployment.

In response to this common problem and a common environment, "virtually every segment of society plunged into public life to advance (or defend) their private values." But many different segments of society acted in many different ways for many different reasons.[169] McCormick focused on some of the major segments of society that have been covered in the recent literature: business and financial interests, industrial workers, farmers, and middle-class women. He described how they variously responded to the common problem of the era: looking to the

---

[168] Richard L. McCormick, "Public Life in Industrial America, 1877 – 1917" in *The New American History*, ed. Eric Foner (Philadelphia: Temple University Press, 1997), 107-132.
[169] In the same volume, Alan Brinkley described the "broad conflict" of the time as the "diverse" responses of various groups that coalesced into a "broad pattern of protest," whereby, "'localistic' people were struggling to preserve control of both the economic and the cultural institutions that governed their lives in the face of encroachments from the modern, bureaucratic order" (137-40). Alan Brinkley, "Prosperity, Depression, and War, 1920 – 1945," in *The New American History*, ed. Eric Foner (Philadelphia: Temple University Press, 1997), 133-158.

government to promote economic growth; organizing and looking to the government to foster unionization and industrial reform; organizing political blocks and cooperative ventures; joining associations and lobbying for reform. McCormick argued that the most notable phenomenon of the era was the organization of socio-political-cultural associations that addressed a wide range of social problems from a wide range of perspectives, and "increasingly offered not panaceas but full-blown agendas for social and political change." In a certain sense these radical, Populist, and Progressive groups failed to achieve much, as decades of historians have shown, but not because they were necessarily naive or ineffective, but because "their enemies were more powerful" and because voting and policy change were seen as the only legitimate form of success. However, McCormick makes clear that reformers of this period were successful in a much larger sense; they were able to create hundreds of organized, "non partisan" associations, which were able to drain "money, manpower, and organizational muscle" from political parties, and in turn "reshaped" the governing system throughout the century along "activist" and "interventionist lines."

The "seeds of Progressivism were planted," McCormick argued, in response to two looming questions: whether social and political institutions were "adequate" enough to address and fix devastating times, and whether "democracy and economic equality were possible in an industrial society?" The Progressives[170] were not alone "in trying to use public, political means to solves problems," but they might have been the most effective and successful group to do so. The Progressive project consisted of four "distinctive methods:" organizing voluntary associations, investigating pertinent problem, finding the facts, and using social scientific analysis to offer a solution. Progressives seemed to believe that experts using the scientific method could find the perfect solutions to all social problems and, further, they believed the solutions would benefit everyone as well as society as a whole. But in reality, Progressives used the rhetoric of science and the common good to mask the imposition of their own values, especially in relation to the "racial and ethnic groups they hated and feared," in their broad efforts to "improve and control the often frightening conditions of industrial life."

---

[170] McCormick noted that the "concept" of "Progressivism" "still dominates the interpretive literature on the early twentieth-century United States" and that for better or worse the "concept is inescapably embedded in the language of contemporaries and the writings of historians." While there were "varied, fervent efforts to solve the problems caused by urbanization and industrialization," the efforts of Progressives were distinctly powerful and long lasting. Progressives were largely native born, urban, middle and upper middle class, and rooted in evangelical Protestantism. They sought to use the social sciences to "eradicate social conflicts" and also to temper the excesses of capitalism (121-22).

Another study of Progressivism was done in 2000 by a political scientist who was engaged on a longitudinal study of a much broader topic. Robert D. Putnam's *Bowling Alone: The Collapse and Revival of American Community* focused on the change of social capital and civic engagement in the United States over the course of the 20th century. In the last section of his book, as a way to set up and inform his policy prescriptions, Putnam devoted a chapter to "Lessons of History: The Gilded Age and the Progressive Era." This chapter was indebted to many of the books reviewed in this paper. In this chapter Putnam praised the "Progressive Era" (which he located from 1900 – 1915) as a good example of "practical civic enthusiasm," but he also said that it was suffused with "exclusion" based on class, ethnicity, and race. Progressives were a "practical" and "experimental" bunch of reformers who shifted programmatically between professionalism and grassroots democracy in their conviction that social, political and economic institutions needed to be better adapted to the modern industrial world – although Putman made it clear that Progressives seemed to prefer "technocratic elitism" and "expert solutions." The main engine of reform was the voluntary association (social, political, religious, and cultural), which was the main focus of Putnam's study. Putnam argued that the period from 1870 to 1920 displayed a "civic inventiveness" in terms of the founding, range, and durability of associational organizations, which was and still is un-paralleled in U.S. history: "to a remarkable extent American civil society at the close of the twentieth century still rested on organizational foundations laid at the beginning of the century." Putnam called Progressivism a "broad and variegated" "social movement" that may not have been much of a social movement in the conventional sense; however, it represented a "civic communitarian reaction to the ideological individualism of the Gilded Age" and the primary form this reaction took was the creation of voluntary associations and socio-political institutions, which greatly increased the aggregate measure of social capital and civic engagement. It was this creation of social capital and civic engagement that marks the Progressive movement as a seminal event in the history of the U.S. and it had an impact many decades after the Progressives as a "movement" faded from the stage. But Putnam ended his chapter with a warning: "social capital is inevitably easier to foster within a homogeneous community." The Progressives' broad expansion of social capital was fostered by systematic socio-political exclusion based on class, ethnicity and race. Putnam praises the Progressive Era for its inventiveness, enthusiasm, and idealism, but warns that its particular reforms "are no longer appropriate for our time" – "Our challenge now is to reinvent the twenty-first-century equivalent."[171]

---

[171] Robert D. Putnam, *Bowling Alone: The Collapse and Revival of American Community* (New York: Simon & Schuster, 2000), 367-401. *The Economist* noted in 2005 that

The last and most recent study to be examined is Michael McGerr's *A Fierce Discontent: The Rise and Fall of the Progressive Movement in America, 1870 – 1920*.[172] This impressively comprehensive book looked at Progressivism in relation to a broad swath of social, political, and cultural responses to industrialization and modernity. Industrialization "fractured old ideologies," wrote McGerr, and "created new ones, including progressivism."[173] Progressives articulated, in the words of one of their figure heads Theodore Roosevelt, a "fierce discontent," and they believed both in social progress and in the moral regeneration of their nation. Progressivism was the "creed of a crusading middle class" that offered the "promise of utopianism" in the wake of industrial inefficiency, urban chaos, political degeneracy, and cultural confusion. Progressivism, McGerr claimed, was a "radical movement" – what he called "the radical center" – that sought not only to "use the state to regulate the economy," but also to "transform" "other social classes," other Americans, into a new socio-cultural body politic. It was this demand for "social transformation," McGerr claimed, that "remains at once profoundly impressive and profoundly disturbing a century later."[174]

McGerr also acknowledged that Progressivism contained many "ambiguities and contradictions," but its various "fault lines" never "split wide open," partly due to the fact that the Progressive middle class was "overwhelmingly white and Protestant" and, for the most part (despite the fissures of class and gender) culturally homogeneous. This raises a central question about which the literature on Progressivism and early 20th century reform has been largely silent until the 1970s, but which many historians since then, including McGerr, have exposed in detail.

"voluntary associations have been the secret ingredient of American social dynamism since the country's foundation…civic associations made Americans better informed, safer, richer and better able to govern themselves and create a just and stable society." This publication commented on Putnam's thesis and argued for new signs of civic participation in the U.S. "The Glue of Society: Americans are Joining Clubs Again," in *A Survey of America*, *The Economist*, 16 July. 2005, 13-17.

[172] Michael McGerr, *A Fierce Discontent: The Rise and Fall of the Progressive Movement in America, 1870 – 1920* (Oxford: Oxford University Press, 2003).

[173] McGerr described the "progressive" ideology as part of the "middle-class alienation from working-class and upper-class culture." He wrote, "Progressivism was the way in which these Victorian men and women came to answer the basic questions of human life that have confronted all people in all times and places: What is the nature of the individual? What is the relationship between the individual and society? What are the proper roles of men, women, and the family? What is the place of work and pleasure in human life?" The answers to these questions "added up to a novel set of guiding values, a new ideology for the middle class: Victorianism gave way to progressivism" – "Rethinking domesticity, rejecting individualism, reconsidering work and pleasure, and redesigning the body" (343 footnote 73, xiv, 42, 64).

[174] Ibid., xiii-xvi, 42, 64, 67-68,

There is a distinct and disturbing relationship between what Nancy MacLean has termed "reactionary populism" and what we have labeled "Progressivism." MacLean's book on the Ku Klux Klan described her subject not as the backwoods yokels they are often mistaken for, but as an organized movement composed of white, evangelical Protestant, mostly petit-bourgeois (but included working class laborers and middle class professionals) who felt threatened by the developments of modernity, and who thereby fomented a reactionary form of populism. The rise of divorce, feminism, black radicalism, white racial liberalism, labor unionization and strikes, monopoly capitalism, and increased immigration are just some of the major issues initiating their conservative reaction.[175] MacLean's Klan members were going through their own status revolution, whereby, the typical Klansmen was economically better off the most blacks and many whites and often upwardly mobile, but still felt "vulnerable," "unstable" and insecure.[176]

Klansmen were conservative, populist, Jacksonian democrats with an explicitly racialized and Protestant conception of White Anglo-Saxon citizenship consecrating white supremacy. They reacted to modernity and industrialization (to the extent that industrialization touched the South) in systematically similar ways to the Progressive programs: both groups formed organized associations; they rhetorically denounced "threats" to their idealized social order; they formulated an ideology to defend an embattled cultural identity; they took action to "reform" or remedy what they considered to be negative socio-political and cultural developments; and they used coercion when rhetorical appeals were not effective. The two main differences between Progressives and reactionary populists were that the Klansmen had an intense distrust of centralized government and statist regulatory authority, and they had a willingness to use violent force[177] as a standard socio-political tactic.

---

[175] Nancy MacLean, *Behind the Mask of Chivalry: The Making of the Second Ku Klux Klan* (Oxford: Oxford University Press, 1994), 79, 33. MacLean argued that one "common core goal" of the Klan was "securing the power of the white petite bourgeoisie in the face of challenges stemming from modern industrial capitalism. The Klan sought to deny political rights to those whom it perceived as threats to that power" (141). MacLean also made it very clear that "extreme conditions" can very easily lead to a "reactionary politics:" "Under conditions of economic uncertainty, sharply contested social relations, and political impasse, assumptions about class, race, gender, and state power so ordinary as to appear 'common sense' to most WASP Americans could be refashioned and harnessed to the building of a virulent reactionary politics able to mobilize millions" (186).

[176] Ibid., 10-11, 52-74.

[177] Ibid., 149-73. MacLean wrote: "Vigilante Violence was the concentrated expression of that culture, of the brutal determination to maintain inherited hierarchies of race, class, and gender that Klansmen sought to conceal with a mask of chivalry" (173).

Another similarity between Progressives and Klansmen was a hierarchical, Social Darwinist belief in the racial and cultural superiority of "white" "civilization," which was often equated with Americanism.[178] C. Vann Woodward pointed out in 1954 that many Americans, including Progressive reformers (living in all areas of the nation, the North, West and South) shared many of the Klansmen's beliefs about a "White" America: "a republic is possible only to men of homogenous race;" the United States of America was "a white man's nation" based on a "white man's religion:" "to stand as impregnable as a tower against every encroachment upon the white man's liberty, the white man's institutions, the white man's ideals, in the white man's country, under the white man's flag."[179] It is no accident of historical fortune that the "Progressive Era" was also the "great age of segregation" in the United States.[180] The Progressives for the most part harbored deep suspicions and prejudices against many groups and social classes that seemed alien to their WASP middle class way of life. Progressive reformers set up hierarchically ordered binary oppositions of identity based on class, race, gender, religion and age. The "fundamental paradox of progressive politics," wrote McGerr, was that Progressives spoke the language of democracy, but in thought and deed they were "not very democratic at all:" the "progressives' condescension toward other groups" created "a narrow definition of 'the people,'" dictated antiparticipatory reforms," "supported disfranchisement," and projected a version of Americanism that was "for whites only."[181] David R. Roediger argued, "The Progressive project of imperialist expansion and the Progressive nonproject of Jim Crow segregation

---

[178] Ibid., 125-48, 166-67; David Roediger, "Whiteness and Ethnicity in the History of 'White Ethnics' in the United States," in *Towards the Abolition of Whiteness: Essays on Race, Politics, and Working Class History* (London: Verso, 1994),189. See also Nell Irvin Painter, *Standing at Armageddon: The United States, 1877 – 1919* (New York: W. W. Norton & Company, 1987): Ch 12.

[179] C. Vann Woodward, *The Strange Career of Jim Crow* (1955; reprint, Oxford: Oxford University Press, 2002), 90-93; Anonymous Klansmen quoted in MacLean, *Behind the Mask of Chivalry*, 132-34, 161; Hofstadter, *The Age of Reform*, 178; John Higham, *Strangers in the Land: Patterns of American Nativism, 1860-1925* (1955; reprint, New Brunswick: Rutgers University Press, 1998) 170-71, 173, 175-77; Nell Irvin Painter, *Standing at Armageddon: The United States, 1877 – 1919*, Ibid; McGerr, *A Fierce Discontent*, 182-218; Dawley, *Struggles for Justice*, 105-38, 254-94; McCormick, "Public Life in Industrial America," 124-26; Brinkley, "Prosperity, Depression, and War," 139-40.

[180] C. Vann Woodward noted in 1954 the related platforms of "Negrophobia and progressivism" in the South: "The omission of the South from the annals of the progressive movement has been one of the glaring oversights of American historians...The blind spot in the Southern progressive record – as, for that matter, in the national movement – was the Negro, for the whole movement in the South coincided paradoxically with the crest of the wave of racism...the typical progressive reformer rode to power in the South on a disfranchising or white-supremacy movement." *The Strange Career of Jim Crow*, Ibid., 90-91.

[181] McGerr, *A Fierce Discontent*, 216-17.

ensured that race thinking would retain and increase its potency."[182] Eric Foner pointed out that Progressives "bore the marks of their nineteenth-century origins" and thus "the idea of 'race' as a permanent, defining characteristic of individuals and social groups retained a powerful hold on their thinking. Consciously or not, it circumscribed the 'imagined community' of Progressive America."[183]

So then what is "Progressivism" and what is the Progressive legacy? These terms are embedded in an "age of social politics."[184] There were many reformist groups of various political and ideological stripes at the turn of the 20th century, of which Progressivism was but one potent example.[185] There were not only many reformist groups that articulated many different reform initiatives, but Progressives also took "man paths" towards reform.[186] As a culturally homogeneous and economically secure social class (although uneasy in their security), Progressive reformers had the ability, education, and socio-economic resources to create many diverse voluntary organizations, which they used to further various social, economic, political, and cultural causes. Progressives were animated on the whole by a Republican-Populist-Protestant infused ideological orientation that often blended capitalist, scientific, and professional methods, all under a politicized and racialized banner of WASP "Americanism."

Progressives sought many types of social change and aligned themselves with various other ideological groups to achieve reform coalitions on specific issues and initiatives, but they were primarily concerned with devising a clear and efficient *order* to harness modernity

---

[182] David R. Roediger, *Working Toward Whiteness: How America's Immigrants Became White* (New York: Basic Books, 2005), 70.

[183] Eric Foner, *The Story of American Freedom* (New York: W. W. Norton & Co., 1998), 185. Foner pointed out many criticisms of the "underside of the Progressives' outlook," like how "their talk of reconstructing society masked a set of managerial attitudes in which democratic values were 'subordinated to technique.'" He also pointed out that because of Progressive's homogenized cultural and racial assumptions, they were "ill-prepared to develop a coherent defense of minority rights against majority or governmental tyranny" (176, 78).

[184] Daniel T. Rodgers, "An Age of Social Politics," in *Rethinking American History in a Global Age*, ed. Thomas Bender (Berkeley: University of California Press, 2002), 250-73.

[185] Michael Kazin argued, "On the national level, it would be hard to disentangle the history of the Left from the history of American reform." He also quoted Will Herberg who wrote, "It would not be too much to say that socialist agitation and propaganda have constituted the single most influential factor in the advance of American social reform. Untiring socialist criticism of existing conditions have invariably served as the main force in opening the way for reform legislation." Michael Kazin, "The Agony and Romance of the American Left," *The American Historical Review*, 100 (Dec 1995): 1510; Will Herberg, "American Marxist Political Theory," *Socialism and American Life*, 1, Donald Drew Egbert and Stow Persons, eds. (Princeton, N.J., 1952): 521.

[186] Foner, *The Story of American Freedom*, Ibid., 141.

and industrialization under the tri-partite *control* of 1) a regulatory State integrated with 2) WASP civic associations and business corporations, and directed by 3) a technocratic elite. "Americanization," to introduce this broad and complicated term which is the central focus of this larger study, could be described as the essential yet myriad conceptualization for this controlling order: "America" as a nationalistic and cultural identity would be the *new order* the Progressives sought and they were very confident, as Gary Gerstle pointed out, "that their use of government and science would turn immigrants into Americans."[187]

As Robert Wiebe argued in "Framing U.S. History: Democracy, Nationalism, and Socialism," the challenge of white Americans during the 18th and 19th century was not to reform so much as to "create a social order" and that social order, my larger study will argue, was a program of Americanization, which included the formation of a federated bureaucracy centered within the corporate-capitalist State. By the early 20th century, this State would come to infuse, unite, and control the parameters of foreign and domestic policy under a neo-liberal rhetoric of welfare capitalism, consumer affluence, and technocratic professionalism.[188] However, the large-scale initiative of Americanization would not be uncontested nor would it be rhetorically or programmatically uniform. As a consensus identity emerged and was inculcated within the public school system, the margins of American society were infused by minority populations who struggled for their own human dignity and opportunity within the American system. The Progressive century of Americanization would be the ideological center of heated debate. Preconceived notions of homogeneous and class based democratic citizenship would be challenged as many minority populations asked, "Who gets to be an American?" – and further, as a socio-cultural-political ideal, "What *ought* America to be?"

---

[187] Gary Gerstle, "Liberty, Coercion, and the Making of Americans," *The Journal of American History* 84:2 (Sept 1997): 530.
[188] Robert Wiebe, "Framing U.S. History: Democracy, Nationalism, and Socialism," in *Rethinking American History in a Global Age*, ed. Thomas Bender (Berkeley: University of California Press, 2002), 236-49.

Cultural War:
Epistemological Authority, Progressive Politics, and the Americanization Movement

The diverse and often contradictory Progressive reform movement has come to characterize an era of "social politics" in U.S. history.[189] At the turn of the 20th century there were many reformist groups with various political and ideological programs (Populists, Progressives, Socialists, anarchists, labor unions, reactionary populists, nativists, and more). Progressivism was the most influential reform ideology of the 20th century because it offered a conservative liberal-capitalist framework for tempering the more radical demands of socialists and labor activists.[190] Not only were there many reformist groups with many different initiatives, but the highly diverse group called the Progressives also took "man paths" of reform.[191] As a relatively culturally homogeneous and economically secure, yet uneasy, social class, what would be later termed the White Anglo-Saxon Protestant (WASP) middle-class, Progressive reformers had the ability, education, and socio-economic resources to create many diverse voluntary organizations, which they used to further various social, economic, political, and cultural causes. Progressives were animated on the whole by a Republican-Populist-Protestant infused ideological orientation that often blended capitalist, scientific, and professional methods, all under a politicized and racialized banner of WASP "Americanism."

---

[189] Daniel T. Rodgers, "An Age of Social Politics," in *Rethinking American History in a Global Age*, ed. Thomas Bender (Berkeley: University of California Press, 2002), 250-73.

[190] Michael Kazin argued, "On the national level, it would be hard to disentangle the history of the Left from the history of American reform." He also quoted Will Herberg who wrote, "It would not be too much to say that socialist agitation and propaganda have constituted the single most influential factor in the advance of American social reform. Untiring socialist criticism of existing conditions have invariably served as the main force in opening the way for reform legislation." Michael Kazin, "The Agony and Romance of the American Left," *The American Historical Review*, 100 (Dec 1995): 1510; Will Herberg, "American Marxist Political Theory," *Socialism and American Life*, 1, Donald Drew Egbert and Stow Persons, eds. (Princeton, N.J., 1952): 521.

[191] Foner, *The Story of American Freedom*, Ibid., 141.

Progressives sought many types of social change and aligned themselves with various other ideological groups to achieve reform coalitions on specific issues and initiatives, but they were primarily concerned with devising a clear and efficient *order* to harness modernity and industrialization under the tri-partite *control* of 1) a regulatory State integrated with 2) WASP civic associations and business corporations, and directed by 3) a technocratic elite.   The idea of "Americanization" could be described as the fundamental yet myriad conceptualization for this controlling order: "America" as a distinct people with a uniform culture and a clear sense of national identity would be the *new order* the Progressives sought and they were very confident, as Gary Gerstle pointed out, "that their use of government and science would turn immigrants into Americans" and, thereby, mold newcomers into the new constructed Progressive American *nation*.[192]

But there is also a disturbing relationship between Progressive reformers and "reactionary populism" that should be addressed. Reactionary populists like Ku Klux Klan members were not the stereotypical backwoods yokel. The Klan was as an organized movement composed of white, evangelical Protestant, mostly petit-bourgeois (but included working class laborers and middle class professionals) who felt threatened by the developments of modernity.   The rise of divorce, feminism, black radicalism, white racial liberalism, labor unionization and strikes, monopoly capitalism, and increased immigration are just some of the major issues initiating their conservative reaction.[193]   Klan members were going through what Richard Hofstadter once called (in a different context) a "status revolution."   Klansmen were economically better off then most blacks and many whites and often upwardly mobile, but they still felt "vulnerable," "unstable" and insecure in their relatively privileged social position.[194]

---

[192] Gary Gerstle, "Liberty, Coercion, and the Making of Americans," *The Journal of American History* 84:2 (Sept 1997): 530.

[193] Nancy MacLean, *Behind the Mask of Chivalry: The Making of the Second Ku Klux Klan* (Oxford: Oxford University Press, 1994), 79, 33. MacLean argued that one "common core goal" of the Klan was "securing the power of the white petite bourgeoisie in the face of challenges stemming from modern industrial capitalism. The Klan sought to deny political rights to those whom it perceived as threats to that power" (141). MacLean also made it very clear that "extreme conditions" can very easily lead to a "reactionary politics:" "Under conditions of economic uncertainty, sharply contested social relations, and political impasse, assumptions about class, race, gender, and state power so ordinary as to appear 'common sense' to most WASP Americans could be refashioned and harnessed to the building of a virulent reactionary politics able to mobilize millions" (186).

[194] Ibid., 10-11, 52-74. Richard Hofstadter, *The Age of Reform, From Bryan to F.D.R.* (New York: Vintage Books, 1955).

Klansmen were conservative, populist, Jacksonian democrats with an explicitly racialized and Protestant conception of White Anglo-Saxon citizenship consecrating white supremacy. They reacted to modernity and industrialization (to the extent that industrialization touched the South) in systematically similar ways to the Progressive programs: both groups formed organized associations; they rhetorically denounced "threats" to their idealized social order; they formulated an ideology to defend an embattled cultural identity; they took action to "reform" or remedy what they considered to be negative socio-political and cultural developments; and they used coercion when rhetorical appeals were not effective. The two main differences between Progressives and reactionary populists were that the Klansmen had an intense distrust of centralized government and statist regulatory authority, and they had a willingness to use violent force[195] as a standard socio-political tactic.

Another similarity between Progressives and Klansmen was a hierarchical, Social Darwinist belief in the racial and cultural superiority of "white" "civilization," which was often equated with Americanism.[196] C. Vann Woodward pointed out in 1954 that many Americans, including Progressive reformers (living in all areas of the nation, the North, West and South) shared many of the Klansmen's beliefs about a "White" America: "a republic is possible only to men of homogenous race;" the United States of America was "a white man's nation" based on a "white man's religion:" "to stand as impregnable as a tower against every encroachment upon the white man's liberty, the white man's institutions, the white man's ideals, in the white man's country, under the white man's flag."[197] It is no accident of historical fortune that the "Progressive Era"

---

[195] Ibid., 149-73. MacLean wrote: "Vigilante Violence was the concentrated expression of that culture, of the brutal determination to maintain inherited hierarchies of race, class, and gender that Klansmen sought to conceal with a mask of chivalry" (173).
[196] Ibid., 125-48, 166-67; David Roediger, "Whiteness and Ethnicity in the History of 'White Ethnics' in the United States," in *Towards the Abolition of Whiteness: Essays on Race, Politics, and Working Class History* (London: Verso, 1994),189. See also Nell Irvin Painter, *Standing at Armageddon: The United States, 1877 – 1919* (New York: W. W. Norton & Company, 1987): Ch 12.
[197] C. Vann Woodward, *The Strange Career of Jim Crow* (1955; reprint, Oxford: Oxford University Press, 2002), 90-93; Anonymous Klansmen quoted in MacLean, *Behind the Mask of Chivalry*, 132-34, 161; Hofstadter, *The Age of Reform*, 178; John Higham, *Strangers in the Land: Patterns of American Nativism, 1860-1925* (1955; reprint, New Brunswick: Rutgers University Press, 1998) 170-71, 173, 175-77; Nell Irvin Painter, *Standing at Armageddon: The United States, 1877 – 1919*, Ibid; McGerr, *A Fierce Discontent*, 182-218; Dawley, *Struggles for Justice*, 105-38, 254-94; McCormick, "Public Life in Industrial America," 124-26; Brinkley, "Prosperity, Depression, and War," 139-40.

was also the "great age of segregation" in the United States.[198]   The Progressives for the most part harbored deep suspicions and prejudices against many groups and social classes that seemed alien to their WASP middle class way of life.   Progressive reformers set up hierarchically ordered binary oppositions of identity based on class, race, gender, religion and age.   The "fundamental paradox of progressive politics," wrote McGerr, was that Progressives spoke the language of democracy, but in thought and deed they were "not very democratic at all:" the "progressives' condescension toward other groups" created "a narrow definition of 'the people,'" dictated antiparticipatory reforms," "supported disfranchisement," and projected a version of Americanism that was "for whites only."[199]   David R. Roediger argued, "The Progressive project of imperialist expansion and the Progressive nonproject of Jim Crow segregation ensured that race thinking would retain and increase its potency."[200]   Eric Foner pointed out that Progressives "bore the marks of their nineteenth-century origins" and thus "the idea of 'race' as a permanent, defining characteristic of individuals and social groups retained a powerful hold on their thinking. Consciously or not, it circumscribed the 'imagined community' of Progressive America."[201]

As Robert Wiebe argued, the challenge of white Americans during the late 18th and 19th century was not to reform so much as to "create a social order" and that social order was a program of Americanization, which included the expansion of a corporate-capitalist State, the dissemination of a WASP nationalism (Americanism), and the trained loyalty of the American public through the public schools and an coordinated civic society.   By the early 20th century, this State would come to infuse, unite, and control the parameters of foreign and domestic policy under a neo-liberal rhetoric of welfare capitalism, consumer

---

[198] C. Vann Woodward noted in 1954 the related platforms of "Negrophobia and progressivism" in the South: "The omission of the South from the annals of the progressive movement has been one of the glaring oversights of American historians…The blind spot in the Southern progressive record – as, for that matter, in the national movement – was the Negro, for the whole movement in the South coincided paradoxically with the crest of the wave of racism…the typical progressive reformer rode to power in the South on a disfranchising or white-supremacy movement." *The Strange Career of Jim Crow,* Ibid., 90-91.

[199] McGerr, *A Fierce Discontent,* 216-17.

[200] David R. Roediger, *Working Toward Whiteness: How America's Immigrants Became White* (New York: Basic Books, 2005), 70.

[201] Eric Foner, *The Story of American Freedom* (New York: W. W. Norton & Co., 1998), 185. Foner pointed out many criticisms of the "underside of the Progressives' outlook," like how "their talk of reconstructing society masked a set of managerial attitudes in which democratic values were 'subordinated to technique.'" He also pointed out that because of Progressive's homogenized cultural and racial assumptions, they were "ill-prepared to develop a coherent defense of minority rights against majority or governmental tyranny" (176, 78).

affluence, and technocratic professionalism.[202] However, the large-scale initiative of Americanization would not be uncontested nor would it be rhetorically or programmatically uniform.   As a consensus identity emerged and was inculcated within the public school system, the margins of American society were infused by minority populations who struggled for their own human dignity and opportunity within the American system. The Progressive project of Americanization would be the ideological center of heated debate over American nationalism, citizenship, and the common good.   The notion of cultural homogeneous, racialized, and class-based democratic citizenship would be challenged as many minority populations. The early 20th century debate focused on, "Who gets to be an American?" and "What *ought* America to be?"

Many white Americans supported a white supremacist view of American nationalism. After the conquest of the Philippines president McKinley wrapped U.S. foreign policy in this doctrine of "the white man's burden." He stated that the Filipinos could not be left to themselves because "they were unfit for self-government" and, thus, the Americans had a duty "to take them all, and to educate the Filipinos, and uplift and civilize and Christianize them, and by God's grace do the very best we could by them." Indiana Senator Albert J. Beveridge believed that the "American Republic" was destined, through the will of God and the dictates of the "highest law" of "race," to be "the most masterful race in history." Nell Irvin Painter explained: "Imperialism was elemental, racial, predestined, for God had prepared the English-speaking people, master organizers, for governing what Beveridge called 'save and senile people.'" Even anti-imperialists, who argued against the trappings of empire for many reasons, often framed their critiques of foreign intervention with the same racist assumptions, and focused more on the implications of empire for poor whites in America. Many Southerners actually felt vindicated by Imperial policies, although skeptical about ruling over more non-white people. Benjamin Tillman argued to his fellows in Congress that "We of the South" had already "borne this white man's burden of a colored race in our midst." In 1883 the Supreme Court had already invalidated the Civil Rights Act of 1875 and by the 1890s there was widespread acceptance of Jim Crow segregation and disenfranchisement laws.   The color line became an increasingly important national preoccupation by the early 20th century as the U.S. became defined more and more as a white man's nation. Thus self-

---

[202] Robert Wiebe, "Framing U.S. History: Democracy, Nationalism, and Socialism," in *Rethinking American History in a Global Age*, ed. Thomas Bender (Berkeley: University of California Press, 2002), 236-49.

proclaimed "progressives" never touched the white supremacy of the South and *de facto* "racial hierarchy" of the country as a whole.[203]

The conservative Progressive Teddy Roosevelt saw the United States as standing on the threshold of "Armageddon" with the evils of plutocratic industrial power on one side and the evils of the violent mob on the other. Under the banners of the "New Nationalism" and the "New Freedom," Roosevelt called for the regulation of society and the economy by an empowered and enlightened federal government which would act as a disinterested arbitrator between conflicting political factions, like labor and capital (of course more radical voices pointed out the impossibility of a disinterested federal government as federal policy was often in the hands of industrial capitalists and their appointed voices in the Congress). Teddy Roosevelt succinctly summarized the ideals of these Progressive reformers: "the object of the government is the welfare of the people. The material progress and prosperity of a nation are desirable chiefly so far as they lead to the moral and material welfare of all good citizens."[204] But as Gary Gerstle has pointed out, Roosevelt's nationalism was based on a racist platform: 1) "political and social equality for all, irrespective of race, ethnicity, or nationality, and a regulated economy that would place economic opportunity and security within the reach of everyone;" 2) the maximizing of "opportunity" for racially superior Americans while also limiting opportunity for racially inferior Americans and immigrants; 3) dealing out "harsh discipline" by means of "marginalization" and "punishment" and/or "Americanization" to "immigrants, political radicals, and others who were thought to imperil the nation's welfare." Rooseveltian nationalism pivoted around a conception of "controlled hybridity" by which both "racial hybridity and purity" and "racial inclusion and exclusion" combined into a more expansive Americanism, but one still marked by racial prejudice, intolerance, and WASP superiority. Roosevelt embraced many of the new European immigrants, both Catholic and Jewish, but he continued to exclude Afro-Americans and Asians from the "crucible" of America. Roosevelt adopted Herbert Croly's conception of "New Nationalism" and used it as a Progressive platform to extend full citizenship only to the new European immigrants on the condition that they left behind their old cultural affiliations to became "100% percent American."[205]

---

[203] Nell Irvin Painter, *Standing at Armageddon: The United States, 1877 – 1919,* Ibid., Ch 5 & 7. See also: George M. Fredrickson, *White Supremacy: A Comparative Study in American and South African History* (Oxford: Oxford University Press, 1981).

[204] Nell Irvin Painter, *Standing at Armageddon: The United States, 1877 – 1919,* Ibid., xxviii, 8, 136, 258, 268.

[205] Gary Gerstle, *American Crucible: Race and Nation in the Twentieth Century* (Princeton: Princeton University Press, 2001): 4-9, 43, 46-51, 71.

Gerstle traces coercive Americanization programs to Theodore Roosevelt's conception of racial nationalism. Roosevelt's conception of "controlled hybridity" allowed for the assimilation of certain ethnic minorities in American only if they completely Americanized by which he meant leaving behind European identity, tradition, and loyalty and taking up American identity, tradition, and loyalty: The immigrant "must not bring in his Old-World religious[,] race[,] and national antipathies, but must merge them into love for our common country, and must take pride in the things which we can all take pride in. He must revere our flag; not only must is come first, but no other flag should ever come second. He must learn to celebrate Washington's birthday rather than that of the Queen or Kaiser, and the Fourth of July instead of St. Patrick's Day…Above all, the immigrant must learn to talk and think and be United States." Roosevelt believed that the duty of the American public school should be to turn immigrants ["hyphenated Americans"] into "Americans pure and simple" because it was "an immense benefit to the European immigrant to change him into an American citizen." He also supported private voluntary associations in their work of Americanizing the immigrant both outside and inside the school.[206]

John Higham traced the origins of early 20th century Americanization efforts to the widespread xenophobia and nativism of the 1890s and earlier. Early forms of nativism congealed into a rampant and rabid nationalist crusade of "America for Americans" and "100 per cent Americanism" during World War I. Fear of the foreigner gave way to a more ambiguous fear of "disloyalty," "the gravest sin in the morality of nationalism," which was any thought that might question the "Absolute and Unqualified Loyalty to Our Country." This search for disloyalty focused uncomfortably on "hyphenated Americans" (German-Americans in particular) and their ability to support not only the war effort, but the greater cause of American nationalism. Infusing the search for disloyalty was a "positive and prescriptive" rhetorical abstraction that did not rise "to the dignity of a systematic doctrine:" "100 per cent Americanism." While there was no specific dogmatic or programmatic ritual to prove one's "Americanism," there were several assumptions underlying this phrase. One was a "belligerent" demand for "universal conformity" to the "spirit of nationalism" and total national loyalty" to

---

[206] Ibid., 53-59, 72, 93-94.

the State, which was regulated through "the pressure of collective judgment." However, "passive assent to the national purpose was not enough; it must be grasped and carried forward with evangelical fervor" through the "inculcation of a spirit of duty:" "Patriotism therefore was interpreted as service." Theodore Roosevelt forcefully supported this sentiment: "We must sternly insist that all our people practice the patriotism of service...for patriotism means service to the Nation...We cannot render such service if our loyalty is in even the smallest degree divided." It was at this time in 1917 that "The American's Creed" ("I pledge allegiance to the flag...") was introduced as a classroom ritual in public schools to remind children of the object of their loyalty, but more so to rhetorically instill the virtue of "right-thinking, i.e. the enthusiastic cultivation of obedience and conformity."[207]

100 per cent Americanism, as Higham argued, was primarily a rhetorical affair of "propaganda" and "exhortation," but with the onset of the war nationalists supported the expansion of state powers and "the punitive and coercive powers" of the state to support if not mandate loyalty and conformity. There were many grass roots level initiatives to suppress German language newspapers, eliminate German from the public school curricula, boycott German opera, and rename German foods (sauerkraut became "liberty cabbage"). There were even many "secret societies" of paralegal militias looking for spies and disloyal subjects. One reported organization was the Anti-Yellow Dog League (supposedly with a thousand affiliated branches), which was made up of adolescent boys over 10 who searched for disloyal Americans. Perhaps the most famous paralegal organization was the American Protective League, which boasted 250,000 members and 1,200 dispersed units. The APL was the Justice Department's "semiofficial" loyalty and conformity watchdog (they even had official badges) composed mostly of middle class professionals and subsidized by corporations. The state and federal governments acted in turn, partly in response to the vitriolic sentiment of the American public. Congress passed an act which repealed the charter of the German-American Alliance and many state governments banned the teaching of German. The Alien Enemies Act of 1798 was revitalized (this statute gave the President "arbitrary" authority over aliens in the U.S. in terms of arresting, restraining, and deporting individuals at will) and the Espionage Act in 1917 was passed (this statue penalized citizens for obstructing the war effort or aiding the enemy via "false statements").

---

[207] John Higham, *Strangers in the Land: Patterns of American Nativism, 1860-1925* (1955; reprint, New Brunswick: Rutgers University Press, 1998): 196, 200, 204-05.

The Sedition Act was passed in 1918, which made any disloyal opinion illegal (whether against the nation, the flag, the government, or the Constitution) and punishable by twenty years in prison. This Act was used extensively against radicals in the U.S. as "any radical critic of the way was customarily designated a 'pro-German agitator.'" As Higham noted, "the new creed of total loyalty outlawed so many kinds of dissent."[208]

As far as the immigrant population in America was concerned there seemed to be a "paradox of American nationalism," which combined both "fraternity" and "hatred." The demands for unity and conformity turned coercive and aggressive mostly towards Germans and radicals, which thereby allowed many immigrant individuals and communities to at least outwardly conform to nationalist purpose and even join the military. As Higham argued, "To a remarkable degree the psychic climate of war gave the average alien not only protection but also a sense of participation and belonging," albeit within an atmosphere of "force of fear and compulsion." This charged atmosphere of 100 per cent Americanism survived and thrived after the war as self-proclaimed Americans still searched out disloyalty. This placed immigrants in a precarious position. The American Legion formed in 1919 in order "To foster and perpetuate a one-hundred-percent Americanism" and ferret out radical agitation. Other "Loyal Legions" and vigilante groups (the second Ku Klux Klan re-emerged in 1915 and grew to several million followers in the 1920s) began to conflate dissolute, radical agitation, and the foreign-born as related problems. The Big Red Scare of 1919 ignited a fever pitch of nationalist hysteria whereby anti-radical nativism began to indiscriminately target immigrant populations, which in turn began to effect industrial labor relations. The Red Scare also pushed zealots like Attorney General Palmer to push for a general sedition law, which would allow for the prosecution of American citizens as well as the foreign born for dissenting opinion. The New York legislature threw out five elected members solely because of their Socialist affiliation. But when Palmer's apocalyptic foretelling of revolution did not materialize on May Day 1920 the country began to realize that there was no widespread internal threat and by the mid-1920s the crest of 100 per cent Americanism began to flow into more peaceful expressions of national fervor.[209]

---

[208] Ibid., 206-23.
[209] Ibid., 215-16, 222-33.

Political liberals of the time did not often disagree with conservative nationalist ideology, except for the more rabid forms of white supremacy and xenophobia. Some liberals did, however, disagree over tactics. By the end of the 19ᵗʰ century liberalism displayed a reformist edge and it organized, as Gary Gerstle has documented, "rational interventions in society and culture," often by turning "to the state as an institutional medium capable of reconstructing society and of educating citizens." Classical liberalism revolved around free markets, limited statism, and bourgeois morality, which often defended corporate capitalism, segregation and disenfranchisement. Progressivism was a three pronged liberal reaction to (a) socialism and labor radicalism, (b) the "extraordinary concentration of power and wealth," and (c) a diverse influx of immigrating ethnic groups. Progressives wanted to find ways to promote and protect "freedom of trade and individual liberty" by way of state regulation and welfare, and by way of "guild socialism." They also wanted to engage in "cultural reconstruction" because liberals believed in the importance of individual moral character as the foundation of civic virtue. When dealing with foreigners this "reconstruction" took the form of "Americanization" in order to "culturally and morally transform...aliens into citizens." But Progressives were a diverse bunch ("left-leaning Progressives" ranging from socialists to left leaning pluralists, and "rightward-leaning Progressives" from Americanizers to hard core nationalists preaching "100 percent Americanism") and because of these conflicts of purposes and methods they "had difficulty fashioning a cultural politics to which they could all adhere," which eventually lead to a loss of "coherence as a political movement."[210] The Americanization movement, however, was an important liberal focus point for first decade of the 20ᵗʰ century. Americanizers ranged from the more conservative and exclusivist "new nationalists" led by Theodore Roosevelt, Herbert Croly, and Frances Kellor, to the more liberal and egalitarian "cosmopolitan pluralists" led by John Dewy, Randolph Bourne, and Jane Addams.

An Americanization movement "emerged" from within the Progressive movement in order to offer "moderate civic nationalist alternatives" to the coercive racial ideology of white supremacists, exclusionists, and nativists that wanted immigration restrictions and limited freedom for immigrants. Noah Pickus defined the

---

[210] Gary Gerstle, "The Protean Character of American Liberalism," *The American Historical Review* 99:4 (Oct 1994): 1043-1073.

Americanization movement in a positive light as "a wide range of legal, political, medical, civic, and cultural efforts to help immigrants adjust to their new surroundings and to encourage Americans to accept them." The Bureau of Naturalization in "An Outline Course in Citizenship" (1916) defined Americanization as the transformation of "uniformed foreigners, not comprehending our language, customs, or governmental institutions, to intelligent, loyal, and productive members of society." The Americanization movement was reacting against the sense of social fragmentation and conflict caused industrial, economic, social and institutional changes and it was made dramatically urgent by the massive influx of immigrants and by the strange newness of a "nationally oriented American society." Progressive reformers felt an urgent need to reorder society and give to all citizens a new "common identity" – a national identity as Americans.[211]

The Americanization movement was concerned with "national unity," but different factions approached this central issue differently. Pickus broke the Americanization movement into two camps: "right-leaning Progressives" like Theodore Roosevelt, Herbert Croly, and Frances Kellor, and "left-leaning Progressives" like John Dewey, Randolph Bourne, and Jane Addams. Both wings offered liberal alternatives to immigrant restriction, but the left wing wanted a pluralist and cosmopolitan "international nation," while the right wing believed in a narrower nationalism that welcomed immigrants only if they "relinquished cultural and political habits thought to be at odds with a robust American identity," and the right wing was willing to use compulsion and force in order to create and preserve the bonds of national unity.[212]

The Americanization movement has been known primarily because of the actions of the more powerful, "mainstream," and influential right-leaning Progressives, and Pickus focused more on this group in his book. Under the banner of "New Nationalism," right-leaning Progressives sought to "eradicate" the ethnic identity of white European

---

[211] Noah Pickus, *True Faith and Allegiance: Immigration and American Civic Nationalism* (Princeton: Princeton University Press, 2005): 64-65, 71-74; Edward George Hartmann, *The Movement to Americanize the Immigrant* (1948; reprint, New York: AMS Press, 1967); John Higham, *Strangers in the Land: Patterns of American Nativism, 1860-1925* (1955; reprint, New Brunswick: Rutgers University Press, 1998); Robert A. Carlson, "Americanization as an Early Twentieth-Century Adult Education Movement," *History of Education Quarterly* 10:4 (Winter 1970): 440-64.
[212] Noah Pickus, *True Faith and Allegiance: Immigration and American Civic Nationalism,* Ibid, 64-65, 73-84 (left-leaning Progressives), 85- 123 (right-leaning Progressives); Jonathan Hansen, "True Americanism: Progressive Era Intellectuals and the Problem of Liberal Nationalism," In *Americanism: New Perspectives on the History of an Ideal,* Michael Kazin and Joseph A. McCartin, eds. (Chapel Hill: The University of North Carolina Press, 2006): 73-89.

immigrants, while disavowing (through silence and segregation) any place for non-white Americans, in order to establish a "uniform national identity" and a fervent sense of patriotism based on WASP principles and culture. Theodore Roosevelt proudly proclaimed in 1906, "We are making a new race" and he later added "The only man who is a good American is an American and nothing else...There is no room in this country for hyphenated Americans." Roosevelt admonished, "The immigrant must learn to talk and think and *be* United States." Nationally the Americanization movement was administrated by the newly formed (1905) Bureau of Naturalization (under the leadership of Commissioner Richard Campbell and his deputy Raymond Crist) and the Bureau of Education (under the leadership of commissioner Philander P. Claxton, Fred Butler, direct of the Americanization Division, and more importantly, Frances Kellor, director of the Division for Immigrant Education, a division completely supported financially by a non-governmental organization, the National Americanization Committee, also lead by Kellor).

Up till the early 1910s the primary method of Americanization had been teaching immigrants how to be "sufficiently American," as Fred Butler asserted, "so that they will not be a danger to us." However, Noah Pickus has noted that Americanizers turned to more "aggressive" methods by the fall of 1915, symbolically demonstrated through the National Americanization Committee's change of slogan from "Many People, But One Nation" to "America First." Frances Kellor and the NAC were very concerned about people not speaking "the same language," not "follow[ing] the same flag," and engaging in "anti-American" activities like "class consciousness and race hatred." Americanization efforts sought to not only make citizens of immigrants, but to make *all* Americans "loyal" with a "respect for authority" because the "security and prosperity" of the nation depended on it. NAC organized and promoted social and industrial programs, military preparedness, coercive educational programs, and recruitment of ethnic leaders, especially members of the ethnic presses. Frances Kellor had wanted to keep Americanization efforts from "alien baiting" and "repressive measures," and she argued that Americanization should also accompany increased economic opportunities for immigrants, but Pickus argued that she was "pushed aside by forces that were committed to an ideologically pure Americans and had no interest in programs that directly aided newcomers." In 1919 the government banned NGO support of government agencies and, thus, NAC support for the Division for Immigrant Education came to an end, and Frances Kellor was removed as national coordinator for Americanization efforts. In 1918 the Bureau of Naturalization had begun to use naturalization fees to publish Americanization textbooks and distribute them as well as establishing the

Division of Citizenship Training led by Deputy Commissioner Raymond Crist. Crist believed that "nearly all can be transformed through attendance at the public schools into desirable citizenship material." He helped coordinate support for Americanization programs in public schools across the nation and by 1922 more than 750 U.S. cities and towns had some type of Americanization program, however, these programs suffered from high drop out rates, dry fact-based textbooks, and reliance on rote memorization and recitation. In 1922 the secretary of labor, James J. Davis, wanted to set up a registration system to force aliens to register for a fee upon entrance to America, and he also wanted mandatory Americanization programs. Davis felt strongly that the U.S. had been "making citizenship entirely too cheap" and he wanted to protect Americans from "contact with the mental, moral and physical delinquents of all the world." He defended his insistence of coercion in the face of critics by arguing, "If we compel the alien to know America, I have no fear that there will come that change of heart necessary to produce an American citizen." The push for more coercive Americanization programs linked Americanization efforts to the simultaneous push by more nativist and reactionary elements for exclusionary immigration policies. However, even these coercive efforts crumbled by the early 1920s as federal, state, and local politicians "proved unwilling to support Americanization programs if doing so required them to provide funding." But Americanization efforts did not die out, instead they expanded and folded into the very fabric of American life and public schooling.[213]

Noah Pickus has argued that left-leaning Progressives did not have a strong enough political "vision" to battle right-wing nationalism and, thus, their "vagueness and confusion" could not put forth a "clear, coherent, [or] compelling moderate alternative position." Thus Americanization devolved into a "zero-sum calculation" that forced immigrants to become "100% American." However, Pickus argued that Americanization was not a "coercive and exclusionary project from its inception." He argued that it was the "fear and insecurity of the war" that helped "legitimate otherwise objectionable policies," and he further argued that part of the reason Americanization efforts collapsed was that "many of its proponents were simply not willing to pursue compulsory assimilatory measures to their logical extremes." Pickus claimed that the "achievements" of the Americanization movement were "remarkable," and he listed four: legislation to protect immigrants, "large-scale practical assistance" to immigrants, outreach programs (including the development of adult education), and improvements to the naturalization system.[214]

---

[213] Ibid., 90-123, 220 (footnote 59).
[214] Ibid., 120-23.

Institutionalizing Progressivism and Americanism: Education Reform and the 'One Best System'

This essay follows close on the heels of our first foray into the historiographical debate over the conceptual terminology of social, cultural, and political "Progressivism." This essay will develop a comprehensive, yet selective portrait of so-called "Progressive" education so as to outline the major ideological and curricular developments that this term (both theory and practice) designates. We will also trace the borders of historiographical debate over the conceptual delineation of Progressive education and, thereby, evaluate its usefulness as a concept for understanding U.S. educational reform programs during the first decades of the 20th century.

The Progressive Education Movement: A Short History

The ideological and curricular roots of Progressive education go back centuries, rooted especially in French and German Romanticism. Early philosophical and educational influences include Jean Jacques Rousseau (1712-1778), Jean Heinrich Pestalozzi (1746-1827), Johann Friedrich Herbart (1776-1834), and Friedrich Froebel (1782-1852). The term Progressive applied to education in the English language seems to have come from Necker *de* Saussure's book *L'Education Progressive, ou Etude du Course de la Vie* (Paris, 1836), which was translated into English in London as *Progressive Education; or, Considerations on the Course of Life* (1839).

American Progressive education is often linked with the earlier nationalist and millennial "propaganda" of the common school reformer Horace Mann, whose mid-19th century common-school movement equated "education" with "national progress." Mann combined "Jeffersonian republicanism," "Christian moralism," and "Emersonian idealism" within his "total faith" in "the power of education." Mann believed universal education would be the "great equalizer" of democratic citizens. He also saw education as a moderating force that would "balance the wheel" of society while also creating "wealth undreamed of." Mann was deeply disturbed by the conflict he saw around him (social, political, economic, and cultural). He wanted a shared national value system that would insure a sense of community and a common political identity. He saw a public, "common" school as the perfect instrument for this mission. But in order to realize this vision of a public school system, Mann had to form "political coalitions" that often united "disparate interests" in a very "political" program of consensus building.[215]

What Horace Mann began, men like William Torrey Harris saw to fruition. When Harris started his work as a school reformer the idea of "universal education" was still very "radical" to most Americans. When Harris had finished his career, universal education "had been made the nub of an essentially conservative ideology." Harris argued for a broader definition of education as a process of socialization that would inculcate children into the local and emerging "national" culture and prepare them for adulthood as democratic citizens. His four basic principles of education were: 1) schooling should prepare children to become lifelong learners as adults; 2) the school should teach only what the child would not be taught by family, friends, and associates; 3) the school should teach only such subject matters as would have "a general theoretical bearing on the world in which the pupil lives;" and 4) the school should teach "moral education," but never "religious education."[216]

The early formation of American Progressive education as a "movement," according to self proclaimed Progressives John Dewey and Robert Holmes Beck, started in Quincy, Massachusetts. It was here that Colonel Francis W. Parker became the superintendent of schools in 1873 and he initiated the "Quincy System" soon thereafter. This new system of education became a quintessential model for what later reformers would label "Progressive." In 1892 the journalist Joseph Mayer Rice ran a series on U.S. public schools for the *Forum*, which was published as a book in 1893, *The Public School System of the United States*. While he did not explicitly mentioning a Progressive educational movement, he did use the term Progressive many times in relation to notable school reforms

---

[215] Lawrence A. Cremin, *The Transformation of the School: Progressivism in American Education, 1876 – 1957* (New York: Vintage Books, 1961), 8-14; Lawrence A. Cremin, *American Education: The National Experience, 1783 – 1876* (New York: Harper & Row, Publishers, 1980), 133-75; Jonathan Messerli, *Horace Mann: A Biography* (New York: Alfred A. Knopf, 1972).

[216] Cremin, *The Transformation of the School*, 14-31; Lawrence A. Cremin, *American Education: The Metropolitan Experience, 1876 – 1980* (New York: Harper & Row, Publishers, 1988), 158-65. In 1871 William Torrey Harris wrote to the Board of Directors of the St. Louis Public Schools: "The spirit of American institutions is to be looked for in the public schools to a greater degree than anywhere else…If the rising generation does not grow up with democratic principles, the fault will lie in the system of popular education."

and initiatives, especially the "Quincy System" of Colonel Parker. Also in 1892, several attendees (including John Dewey) of the National Education Association meeting in Saratoga Springs, New York formed the National Herbart Society to promote the educational philosophy of the famous German pedagogue. A year later G. Stanley Hall published his first major research project on child study, "The Contents of Children's Minds" (1893). This research subject would eventually feed into a larger child study movement that would become the major plank of the Progressive education platform: child-centered curriculum and instruction.[217]

A Progressive educational "movement" was said to have stirred in earnest by the time John Dewey began his "Laboratory School" in Chicago in 1896 and gave his lectures on *The School and Society* in 1899. The movement supposedly congealed between the founding of the Association for the Advancement of Progressive Education (or the Progressive Education Association, PEA) in 1919 and its publication of *Progressive Education* starting in 1924. The high-water mark for Progressive education in terms of organizational development and theoretical vitality was during the 1930s. An impassioned organ of radical Progressive educational theory and practice, *The Social Frontier*, appeared in print in 1934 as an outlet for Social Reconstructionist thought. Due to financial insolvency, it was later tempered and incorporated into the PEA as *Frontiers of Democracy*, which ran from 1939 to 1944. In 1936 many influential Progressive educators and intellectuals formed the John Dewey Society as a moderate forum to discuss Progressive and liberal philosophy. The John Dewey Society also started to publish important educational research yearbooks by 1937.

1938 might have marked the apex of Progressivism in the U.S. In this year the Progressive Education Association's enrollment peaked at 10,440 members; *Time* magazine featured the PEA as a cover story and announced its wide influence; and John Dewey and Boyd Bode both warned fellow Progressives that the movement was dissolving into a non-political, child-centered libertarianism instead of a comprehensive movement for social democracy.[218] However, despite its organizational success, the actual impact of Progressive innovations on American education by the 1930s is uncertain. The celebratory framework of most reformist

---

[217] Cremin, *The Transformation of the School*, 355-58; Herbert M. Kliebard, *The Struggle for the American Curriculum, 1893-1958*, 3rd ed (1986; reprint, New York: RoutledgeFalmer, 2004): 1-25.

[218] John Dewey, *Experience and Education* (New York: Macmillan, 1938); Boyd Bode, *Education at the Crossroads* (New York: Newson, 1938).

literature has obscured more concrete evaluations by later historians.[219] C.A. Bowers pointed out that due to Progressive educator's focus on elementary school teachers and classrooms, "the influence of the Progressive education movement was restricted to only a fraction of the nation's 1 million teachers" – although he argued that one should not discount the wide influence of Progressive intellectuals in teacher training Education departments. Bowers estimated that William H. Kilpatrick taught almost 35,000 students between 1909 and 1938. Larry Cuban has made one estimate of Progressive influence on the practice of public schooling. He argued that at its peak (between 1920-40) no more than 25% of New York public school teachers "adopted Progressive teaching practices, broadly defined, and used them to varying degrees in the classrooms." David Tyack, Robert Lowe, and Elisabeth Hansot argued that, overall, actual Progressive reform in public schools was a mixed bag, and to the extent that concrete Progressive reforms were initiated and retained over a long period of time, they "fared best in relatively prosperous states and districts" and "most affected children from favored social classes. Ironically, of course, these were the groups least in need of help."[220]

---

[219] There were several early histories of Progressive education that were produced while the movement was still widely influential, but they were written primarily by Progressive educators who had an obvious interest in writing the history of their own cause. The first was Edward H. Reisner's "What is Progressive Education?" in *Teachers College Record* (1933-4) and then Merle Curti's *The Social Ideas of American Educators* (1935). A few years later R. Freeman Butts published *The College Charts Its Course* (1939). Robert Holmes Beck wrote the first dissertation on Progressive education at Yale University in 1941, "American Progressive Education, 1875 – 1930." The last early history of the movement written by a partisan was Harold Rugg's *Foundations for American Education* (1947). C.A. Bowers reported in 1969 that "most of the sources that deal with Progressive education are books and articles written by professors of education. Unfortunately, they proved little help in determining how widely their contents were accepted among classroom teachers." Bowers stated the "desirability" of a study on "how much influence the theoreticians actually had on the practitioners in the classroom." *The Progressive Educator and the Depression: The Radical Years* (New York: Random House, 1969), x.

[220] Cremin, *The Transformation of the School*, 355-58; Larry Cuban, *How Teachers Taught: Constancy and Change in American Classrooms, 1890 – 1980* (New York: Longman, 1993), 75; Bowers, *The Progressive Educator and the Depression*, 11; David Tyack, Robert Lowe, and Elisabeth Hansot, *Public Schools in Hard Times: The Great Depression and Recent Years* (Cambridge, MA: Harvard University Press, 1984): 152, 158. Tyack et. al. also note: "To the degree that Progressive educators succeeded in retaining old programs or installing new ones, they had to work within severe fiscal constraints in most districts. And the success of publicized reforms probably obscured the conservatism of the great mass of American public schools."

It is important to note in more detail the radical group of Progressive educators that organized as a block during the 1930s in opposition to capitalism and New Deal liberalism. They called themselves "Social Reconstructionists" and they were the radical wing of the Progressive education movement. The intellectual catalyst and the most important spokesman for this group was George S. Counts whose call to arms – "Dare Progressive Education Be Progressive?" – was unleashed in 1932. Taking inspiration from radical social scientists like Charles Beard and Thorstein Veblen, as well as the broader socialist movement, Counts published the first manifesto for the Social Reconstructionist platform in 1932, *Dare the School Build a New Social Order?*, which was shortly followed by *The Social Foundations of Education* (1934) and the more tempered writings of William H. Kilpatrick, *Education and the Social Crisis* (1932) and his edited volume of radical Progressive thought *The Educational Frontier* (1933). Most of the social reconstructionists were first active members of the PEA, but between 1931 and 1933, these radicals expressed their desire for more militant social reform through education in the pages of *Progressive Education* and within PEA committees – most notably the Committee on Social and Economic Problems and its publication, *A Call to the Teachers of the Nation* (1933). After Counts self-consciously raised the ideological banner of Social Reconstruction, he helped found *The Social Frontier* in 1934, which was then the official organ for radical Progressive thought and became a marked contrast to the more moderate views found in *Progressive Education.* According to C. A. Bowers, the social Reconstructionist faction rose to prominence in the wake of the Great Depression and took control of the Progressive education movement by 1947, although by then they espoused a more moderate platform based on democratic values, like deliberation and "democratic living." But of course, by this time Progressive education was becoming an embattled cause.[221]

By the late 1940s and early 1950s both wings of Progressive education were under widespread attack as the cultural climate in the U.S. narrowed its horizons and punished unpopular opinions. By mid-century, America was becoming a very "counterprogressive"

---

[221] David Tyack, Robert Lowe, and Elisabeth Hansot have succinctly criticized the Social Reconstructionist agenda: "The reconstructionists challenged the existing order by a powerful alternative vision of America, but their strategy seemed naïve to many radicals, their goal seemed dangerous to many conservatives, and their grasp of educational realities seemed tenuous to many fellow school people. Socialism was the road not taken." *Public Schools in Hard Times: The Great Depression and Recent Years*, 47-48.

country.[222]   Lawrence Cremin noted, "The surprising thing about the Progressive response to the assault of the fifties is not that the movement collapsed, but that it collapsed so readily."   In 1951 David Hullburd published *This Happened in Pasadena* chronicling the demise of Pasadena's Progressive superintendent Willard Goslin. John Dewey died in 1952.   The Progressive Education Association collapsed by 1955. *Progressive Education* (financed by the John Dewey Society after the end of the PEA) issued its last publication in July, 1957.   And the John Dewey Society published its last yearbook in 1962 (but the organization remains active to date).   Despite the speedy demise of the movement within a decade, Lawrence Cremin was somberly optimistic about its importance.   In 1961 he noted, "the transformation" Progressive educators were able to achieve in the school system "was in many ways" "irreversible." He hinted that Progressive education would be back, if in fact it ever completely left: "the authentic Progressive vision remained strangely pertinent" – perhaps "awaiting" a "reformulation and resuscitation that would ultimately derive from a larger resurgence of reform in American life and thought." Cremin uttered these words quite self-consciously as the first comprehensive chronicler of the history Progressive education.[223]

---

[222] Peter Novick, *That Noble Dream: The "Objectivity Question" and the American Historical Profession*, 332, 370. Novick used the term "counterprogressive" to characterize primarily the change of interpretive framework within the historical community, which was reacting against the Progressive historiography of Charles Beard and Carl Becker. But he also extended its use to include the reaction against Progressive educationalists like John Dewey: "By the 1950s counterprogressivism extended to the conviction that John Dewey had had a pernicious influence on American education, and that to combat 'populist' anti-intellectualism, one had to return to a more traditional curriculum, and restore the authority of academic elites." C. A. Bowers noted, "A heavy barrage of criticism was being leveled at Progressive education by an awakened and highly concerned public. Dissatisfaction with Progressive education had been growing among interested and vocal members of the American public since the early forties, but it was not until 1949 that they began a direct assault on the philosophy and practice of Progressive schools. The attack was so sweeping that little escaped condemnation." *The Progressive Educator and the Depression*, 242.
[223] Ibid., 347-53; Daniel Tanner, *Crusade for Democracy: Progressive Education at the Crossroads* (New York: State University of New York Press, 1991). C. A. Bowers, *The Progressive Educator and the Depression*, 242. Bowers noted: "The idea that the schools should be used to overcome the problems of racial integration, a high divorce rate, and chronic poverty, as well as to help American beat the Russians to the moon indicates that at least part of the social reconstructionist philosophy of education has become accepted as the 'conventional wisdom' of our society" (253).

Historiography of The Progressive Education Movement

As an academic pursuit in the United States, the History of Education is a relatively new field of study. It has been around for only about 100 years and it is still arguably fighting for its status as a major disciplinary category of history. It was originally linked to the Philosophy of Education in the late 19th century and began to emerge on its own with the publication of *Source Book of the History of Education for the Greek and Roman Period* (1901), which was written by a sociologist named Paul Monroe. Monroe was asked to research the History of Education by the Dean of Teachers College at Columbia University, James Earl Russell, and Monroe would write several volumes thereafter. Due to Monroe's work, the History of Education emerged as a disciplinary field of study. The first institution to offer doctoral degrees in History of Education was Teachers College at Columbia University. Teachers College alumni produced several influential dissertations on the History of Education during the first two decades of the 20th century.[224]

It was Ellwood Patterson Cubberley, the first dean of the School of Education at Stanford University, who took hold of the History of U.S. Education and strove to make it not only a thriving academic discipline, but also a professional "science." His monumental work toward this end was *Public Education in the United States* (1919). It was an important early contribution toward the so-called "scientific" history of the early 20th century, although it suffered from the same flawed conceptions of "science" and "objectivity" as did other "scientific" works of history that emerged at the time.[225] Under the rhetoric of "science," Cubberley's work suffered from a selective and celebratory "Whig" interpretation of educational history and was used as a campaign tool for his own part in the Progressive educational crusade. Despite the efforts of scholars like Cubberley, the History of Education remained a small sub-field for the first half of the 20th century and most of the major organs of historical research, including the American Historical Association, would publish only a few articles on the subject.[226]

It was not until the 1960s and the breakthrough scholarship of Bernard Bailyn and Lawrence A. Cremin, combined with the launching of the journal *History of Education Quarterly*, that the History of

---

[224] Thomas Woody earned his PhD in the History of Education in 1918 at Teachers College and went on to become an early and prolific writer of educational history. He wrote many books on the history of education, both European and American. James Mulhern, "Perspectives," *History of Education Quarterly* 1 (June 1961): 1-4.

[225] Peter Novick, *That Noble Dream: The "Objectivity Question" and the American Historical Profession* (Cambridge: Cambridge University Press, 1988).

[226] Ellen Condliffe Lagemann, "Does History Matter in Education Research? A Brief for the Humanities in an Age of Science," *Harvard Educational Review* 75 (Spring, 2005), 9-24.

Education became a respected sub-field within the academy.[227] By this time the historical community was going through a transvaluation of values, as professional and epistemological standards were changing. Much of the new history and historiography of U.S. education challenged old Whiggish pieties and introduced a much more complicated, fragmented, and often radical critique of American education. The 1960's historiographical debate within the history profession, especially within the education community, stoked the flames of a cultural divide that would fulminate into the 21st century.[228]

One of the seminal works of this formative period was *The Transformation of the School: Progressivism in American Education, 1876 – 1957* (1961) by Lawrence Cremin. It was an important and still is in many ways an unsurpassed study of the history of Progressive education.[229] In this prizewinning book[230] Cremin tried to sketch a full picture of not only the educational and theoretical principles of the movement, but also its intellectual and historical generation. Like last chapter's survey of the historiographical literature on the larger conception of "Progressivism," we will now focus particularly on various conceptions of Progressive education so as to get some clarity about the

---

[227] The History of Education Society transformed an earlier publication, *History of Education Journal*, which was founded in 1951 under the editorship of Claude Eggertson, into a more academic organ with the launching of *History of Education Quarterly* in 1961 under the editorship of Ryland W. Crary at the University of Pittsburgh.

[228] For historiographical debate see Novick, *That Noble Dream*; Robert Harrison, "The 'new social history' in America" in *Making History: An Introduction to the History and Practices of a Discipline*, ed. Peter Lambert and Phillipp Schofield (London: Routledge, 2004): 109-20; Peter Charles Hoffer, "Part I: Facts and Fictions" in *Past Imperfect: Facts, Fictions, Fraud – American History from Bancroft and Parkman to Ambrose, Bellesiles, Ellis, and Goodwin* (New York: PublicAffairs, 2004): 11-130; Gary B. Nash, Charlotte Crabtree, and Ross E. Dunn, *History on Trial: Culture Wars and the Teaching of the Past* (1997; reprint, New York: Vintage Books, 2000). For some specific mention of this debate within educational historiography see Diane Ravitch, *The Revisionists Revised: A Critique of the Radical Attack on the Schools* (New York: Basic Books, 1978); Jeffrey E. Mirel, "Introduction" in William J. Reese, *Power and the Promise of School Reform: Grassroots Movements During the Progressive Era* (1986; reprint, New York: Teachers College Press, 2002): ix-xvi; Herbert M. Kliebard, "Afterword: The Search for Meaning in Progressive Education: Curriculum Conflict in the Context of Status Politics" in *The Struggle for the American Curriculum, 1893 – 1958*, 3rd ed (New York: RoutledgeFalmer, 2004).

[229] C.A. Bowers called Cremin's book "the most important history of the Progressive education movement, particularly in its early phases." *The Progressive Educator and the Depression*, 259. Hebert M. Kliebard argued, "Cremin succeeded in establishing history of education as an integral part of cultural and social history, and the writing of history of education has never really been the same since his book appeared." *The Struggle for the American Curriculum*, 272. On the 30th anniversary of the work, John L. Rury argued that the book's "appearance did much to make educational history a credible subfield of American history, and one open to new research and interpretation." "Transformation in Perspective: Lawrence Cremin's Transformation of the School," *History of Education Quarterly* 31 (Spring 1991): 66-76.

[230] It won the Bancroft Prize in American History in 1962.

meaning and significance of the term "Progressive" as it related to education and educational reform. Thus, we will be restricting our historiographical discussion to one central question: What was Progressive education? To the extent that Americanization was involved within the Progressive educational program, it will be mentioned as a topical subject, but a full analysis of the history and meaning of Americanization programs and a review of the literature on this topic will come later in the chapter.

In *The Transformation of the School*, Cremin was quite clear that Progressive education was a "many-sided effort" and "marked from the very beginning by a pluralistic, frequently contradictory, character." He cautioned his reader that he would offer no "capsule definition of Progressive education" because "none exists, and none ever will; for throughout its history Progressive education meant different things to different people." However, with this caution in mind, Cremin offered several definitions with which one could define this movement. Progressives were "moderate" reformers who believed in democracy and wanted to use education as "an adjunct to politics in realizing the promise of American life." He described Progressive education as "part of a vast humanitarian effort to apply the promise of American life – the ideal of government by, of, and for the people – to the puzzling new urban-industrial civilization that came into being during the later half of the nineteenth century." As such it was a "many-sided effort to use the schools to improve the lives of individuals" in four distinct ways: (1) a "broadening" of the school to meet and treat all areas of the community; (2) applying the new "scientific" research of educational professionals inside the classroom; (3) reshaping a student centered curriculum to meet the needs of a diverse study body; (4) instilling a "radical faith that culture could be democratized" and thereby training responsible citizens to lead the country to progress and prosperity. A quintessential expression of the Progressive ethos came from Jane Addams, who Cremin quoted in his introduction: "We have learned to say that the good must be extended to all of society before it can be held secure by any one person or any one class; but we have not yet learned to add to that statement, that unless all men and all classes contribute to a good, we cannot even be sure that it is worth having."[231]

Cremin argued that Progressive education and its pedagogical agenda could best be defined by summarizing the seven founding principles of the Association for the Advancement of Progressive Education (or PEA). PEA's 1919 statement of purpose proclaimed, "The aim of Progressive Education is the freest and fullest development of the individual, based upon the scientific study of his mental, physical, spiritual, and social characteristics and needs." The principles of this

---

[231] Cremin, *The Transformation of the School*, viii-x, 88-89.

organization included: (1) children should be free to naturally develop according to both individual self-expression and the social needs of the community; (2) the learning process should include a) hands-on direct experience, b) a holistic conception of knowledge and its practical application, as well as c) self-reflexivity; (3) the teacher should guide the social and intellectual development of the child and this necessitates a) a well trained and creative teacher, b) a stimulus-rich learning environment, and c) small class sizes; (4) learning assessments should include both "objective and subjective reports" on the "physical, mental, moral, and social" aspects of the child's development; (5) the overall wellbeing and health of the student is a primary concern; (6) the school should communicate and cooperate with the home in educational, developmental, and extracurricular endeavors; (7) the Progressive school should be a "laboratory" of "new ideas" and it should take the lead in educational initiative.[232]

Cremin also evaluated the specific impacts of Progressive initiatives within the U.S. public school system. He listed 10 points of measurable change: (1) an "extension" of education on all levels whereby more and more children were steadily attending kindergartens on through high school; (2) school system shifted to six years in elementary, three years in junior high, and three years in high school; (3) a "continuing expansion and reorganization of the curriculum at all levels;" (4) expansion of extracurricular activities; (5) "more variation and flexibility in the grouping of students;" (6) the learning environment – classroom – became more active, informal and mobile; (7) teaching materials, including textbooks, expanded to increase the interest and learning of the student; (8) the architecture of schools changed to accommodate gymnasiums, playgrounds, athletic fields, and such; (9) teachers became better trained and certified – in word, professionalized; (10) school administration became more centralized, professionalized, and bureaucratic.[233]

There were also some notable failures of Progressive education as well, which Cremin noted: (1) because of success and the diversity of its practitioners, it eventually suffered from schisms and the distortion of its comprehensive aims; (2) Progressives were better able to articulate "what they were against than what they were for;" (3) Progressive reforms often demanded too much time and ability from teachers; (4) after reforms were initiated, Progressives were often tied to specific programs and could not "formulate next steps;" (5) a failure to adequately

---

[232] Ibid., 240-45.
[233] Ibid., 306-8.

deal with the conservative post-war climate; (6) professionalization of educators and administrators brought isolation from reform coalition partners in the public who were key in backing and initiating reform programs; and finally, Cremin argued, (7) Progressive educators became to attached to Progressive initiatives and too detached from the "continuing transformation of American society."[234]

In the third volume of Lawrence Cremin's award winning series,[235] *American Education: The Metropolitan Experience, 1876 – 1980* (1988), he revisited his definition of "education" and how its meaning in the American context was tied to both nationalism and reformism. In this volume Cremin noted that by the late 19th century education was becoming increasingly valued by the public at large and so educational reforms were becoming increasingly political conflicts. But at the same time, Cremin pointed out, the "American *paideia*" had not been not settled or formalized and, thus, "Americans were still in the process of defining what it meant to be an American." However, this did not stop the growing corporate state and its elite WASP representatives from fashioning their own version of American identity as an Anglo Saxon "manifest destiny," which was being actively carried over the continent and across the seas as a form of "cultural imperialism" (accompanying, of course, more traditional forms of economic and political imperialism as well). But struggling alongside this push for a dominant American *paideia* modeled on WASP cultural values were "alternative American paideias" fomented by African Americans, Native Americans, and immigrant communities. This created a "complicated" educational terrain as competing socio-cultural groups fought over the right to transmit their own diverse cultural value systems.

It is within this context that "Americanization" programs were launched both within and outside of the pubic school system by mostly Progressive forces. The arch-purpose of these programs was to bring a homogenized ideological order to the newly conceived "nation" and, thereby, solidify a dominant American identity with which to inculcate both children and adults so as to "assimilate" the population into what Progressive reformers believed to be *the* "dominant American community." But Cremin also noted the "pluralistic" character of the many (often "contradictory") Progressive "movements," and thus he dwelt a great deal on how Progressivism also contained a strand of

---

[234] Ibid., 347-51.
[235] The second volume, *American History: The National Experience, 1783 – 1876*, was awarded the Pulitzer Prize for History in 1981.

"liberalism" that sought to "democratize the concept of culture" and promote an "inclusive politics" that addressed the "problems of inequality" within the U.S.[236]

The last work by Lawrence Cremin that we will note is "Education as Politics," a lecture given in 1989. Cremin made it clear (within the highly charged standards and multicultural educational debates of the 1980s) that "education has always served political functions." More specifically, he claimed the educational endeavor eternally focuses on the "future character of the community" and to that extent education can never be separated from politics: "It is impossible to talk about education apart from some conception of the good life; people will inevitably differ in their conceptions of the good life, and hence they will inevitably disagree on matters of education; therefore the discussion of education fall squarely within the domain of politics."

Cremin argued that U.S. education has always been politicized, especially by Progressive reformers, but he tried to make the argument that it became "increasingly politicized" in the wake of Progressivism, post WWII, as many diverse groups "with differing conceptions of the good life" escalated the battle over "the nature and character of education." These battles ensued, Cremin pointed out, because of a longstanding U.S. Progressive tradition to use the system of education to try and "solve" all sorts of socio-political problems, "and in so doing to invest education with all kinds of millennial hopes and expectations." Cremin mentioned social critics like Hannah Arendt who pointed out that educational systems are limited in their ability to change the world, yet she noted that this has not stopped successive waves of Americans from trying to use education for just that purpose.[237] When people battle over educational systems and curriculum, Cremin argued, they are really debating "alternative views of the good life," especially what "kind of America they would prefer to live in and what it might mean to be an American."

Cremin believed Dewey to be the great philosopher of American social and political ideals in relation to its educational practices, but Dewey was not the only intellectual force to make the connection

---

[236] Lawrence A. Cremin, *American Education: The Metropolitan Experience, 1876 – 1980* (New York: Harper & Row, 1988), 10-14, 110, 150, 178, 196, 228, 442-44. Cremin also used the term "American Victorianism" to describe the Americanization program of "standardizing" culture based on "ethnic, religious, and racial ethnocentrism" so as to "convey its outlook upon the world and thereby enforce its standards and patterns of behavior" (442-44).
[237] Cremin quoted Hannah Arendt, "The Crisis in Education," *Partisan Review* (Fall 1958): 494-95.

between education and politics. Cremin argued that a "distinctively American paideia" molded out of WASP values, nationality, and patriotism became the norm during the 19th century and it demanded a "relentless" program for cultural and political "assimilation:" "the more different the newcomers from the British-American model, the more intense the manifestations of concern." But the process and programs of "Americanization," Cremin argued, did not have the desired effect. First of all, for all the rhetoric of a unified WASP paideia, it was never completely realized, and it was often "loosely and variously defined:" The American norm to which school children were "supposed to be assimilating often proved confusing and elusive." Second, the American paideia began to change in relation to the ever evolving context of American society. And finally, deep seated racism in all parts of the U.S. gave rise to many severe restrictions and rejections of specific minority communities based on their assumed inferiorities. This in turn gave rise to many protest movements over the course of the 20th century and a vigorous debate over "precisely what it meant to be an American." Cremin ended his essay by noting that American identity has always "inevitably depend[ed]" on the complex and changing "interaction" of the diverse U.S. population. He also reiterated the limited, yet central, role of education within past and present debates on Americanism: "Education cannot take the place of politics, though it is inescapably involved in politics, and education is rarely a sufficient instrument for achieving political goals, though it is almost always a necessary condition for achieving political goals."[238]

If Lawrence Cremin was the first major historian of U.S. education, his seminal reputation was eclipsed not a generation later by the work of David B. Tyack, professor of Education and History at Stanford University. Tyack has authored and co-authored a host of seminal works that have focused on various reform initiatives during the 19th and 20th centuries. We will be surveying several of his major works.

His first major book was *The One Best System: A History of American Urban Education* (1974). This book focused on the "politics" of education by which Tyack meant "who got what, where, when, and how." Tyack wanted to study not only the decision makers who initiated reform, but also those segments of the American population (the "poor and dispossessed) who were marginalized from the political process and, thereby, often the passive recipients of reform programs. Being largely left out of political decisions, the poor were often "victimize[ed]" "predictab[ly] and regular[ly]" by "systematic" reform initiatives that were not drafted or implemented in their interests. And further, these

---

[238] Lawrence A. Cremin, "Education as Politics" in *Popular Education and Its Discontents* (New York: Harper & Row, 1990), 85-127. The three essays in this book were based on lectures given at the Harvard Graduate School of Education in 1989.

"victims" of systematic injustice were often blamed for their own marginalization. In framing his discussion around the issue of justice, Tyack's study invoked (while criticizing) Progressive principles. He primarily sought to expose the "systemic injustice" at the root of Progressive reforms, which meant a focus not on individuals per se but on the institutions within the "social system" that created and reinforced an atmosphere of injustice:

> It is more important to expose and correct the injustice of the social system than to scold its agents. Indeed, one of the chief reasons for the failures of educational reforms of the past has been precisely that they called for a change of philosophy or tactics on the part of the individual school employee rather than systemic change – and concurrent transformations in the distribution of power and wealth in the society as a whole...Despite frequent good intentions and abundant rhetoric about "equal educational opportunity," schools have rarely taught the children of the poor effectively – and this failure has been systematic, not idiosyncratic. Talk about "keeping the schools out of politics" has often served to obscure actual alignments of power and patterns of privilege. Americans have often perpetuated social injustice by blaming the victim, particularly in the case of institutionalized racism...The search for conspiracies of villains is a fruitless occupation; to the extent that there was deception, it was largely self-deception. But to say that institutionalized racism, or unequal treatment of the poor, or cultural chauvinism were unconscious or unintentional does not erase their effects on children.

Tyack was also lending his skills as a scholar toward a broader initiative of "social justice," which he argued (also working out of a Progressive conception) could be found "in the old goal of a common school, reinterpreted in radically reformed institutions."[239]

Tyack looked mostly at the urban reforms of a growing urban society. Administrative Progressives believed that the older systems of rural schools in the U.S. were too haphazardly organized, inefficient, substandard, and too "subordinated" to community interests. Reformers, especially urban reformers, thought that rural communities were backwards and ignorant of the complex needs of modern society.

---

[239] David B. Tyack, *The One Best System: A History of American Urban Education* (Cambridge, MA: Harvard University Press, 1974), 3-12.

Progressive reformers "blended economic realism with nostalgia, efficient professionalism with evangelical righteousness" so as to initiate a complex re-ordering, nationalization, and professionalization of the public school system. They wanted to engineer the "one best system" of education that could create a "standardized, modernized 'community' in which leadership came from the professionals." While cloaked in the rhetoric of democracy, the needs of society, and the education of all, Progressive school reforms in urban areas were more about reconstituting the nature of authority in order to "transfer of power from laymen to professionals," and thereby, create a nationalized (and standardized) educational bureaucracy. The results of this restructuring did lead to "better school buildings, a broader and more contemporary course of studies, and better qualified teachers and administrators," while also giving "country youth greater occupational mobility" and introducing them to "different life-styles."[240]

But there was also a darker side to urban reforms. In a search for the "one best system," administrative Progressives continually stressed "order" and "standardization." It was a program of "institutionalization" to combat the social chaos of modernity in urban America. William T. Harris, superintendent of schools in St. Louis, asserted in his *School Report for 1871*, "The first requisite of the school is Order: each pupil must be taught first and foremost to conform his behavior to a general standard."[241] School modernization and professionalization was modeled on the factory system of bureaucratic division of labor and it often reinforced principles like punctuality, chain of command, coordination, systematizing, hierarchical organization, impersonal rules, regularized procedures, objective standards, efficiency, rationality, and precision. In some cases reformers sought professional bureaucracies so as to promote a more equalized "meritocracy" that would serve all segments of the urban community impartially and fully. However, the "rational" bureaucratic systems of education often "reinforced racial, religious, and class privilege," as well as normalizing "subordination" of students and teachers to the authority of white, male school administrators. WASP professionals simply assumed that their values and interests as "honest and competent experts" were universal goods and, thus, under their control "public education was the most human form of social control and the safest method of social renewal." [242]

Prefiguring a later book, David Tyack and Elisabeth Hansot published "From Social Movement to Professional Management:

---

[240] Ibid., 19-27.
[241] Tyack quoted William T. Harris, *St. Louis School Report for 1871*, 31-32.
[242] Ibid., 28-43, 60-65, 72-77, 109, 127-131, 146-47.

An Inquiry into the Changing Character of Leadership in Public Education" (1980). In this article Tyack and Hansot "interpret[ed] changing forms of leadership in public education" from the 19th to the 20th centuries. The common school reformers largely shared a "Protestant-republican ideology" and engaged in an evangelical process of "nation building" through a "millennial" crusade to create a "righteous society." Common school reformers were lead by charismatic leaders whose main tools were exhortation and persuasion based on a shared Protestant-republican ideology: "leadership in public education largely took the form of guiding a decentralized social movement because the chief task was the *creation* of common schools through the mobilization of opinion and effort at the local level." 20th century reformers believed in "social efficiency," by which they meant organizational reforms resulting in "new structures and processes of schooling that would enable public education to mesh smoothly and efficiently with a corporate society." These professional school men sought to "take the school out of politics" by centralizing school authority, consolidating children in larger schools, standardizing curriculum, and normalizing a bureaucratic-business model of education: "Believing that the basic structure of society was just and Progressive, the new leaders thought that they knew how to bring about a smoothly running, socially efficient, and stable society in which education was the major form of human engineering."

Tyack and Hansot emphasized that these two movements were "not so sharply distinct" and that there was "significant overlap between the two eras." Both movements shared in the continuity of organizational structuring and expansion that started with the common school leadership. Tyack and Hansot argue that the grass-roots initiated common school movement was the "most impressive case of institution building in American history." Its success was largely due to a homogeneous leadership core, which shared similar ideological orientations and social and economic interests. These reformers wanted to create a national system of Christian common schools in which a "Protestant *paideia*" would "express and perpetuate" their shared socio-cultural values and "civic purpose." Tyack and Hansot argued that part of the "genius" of this movement "was that its leaders were able to wrap their cause in a noncontroversial Americanism," which legitimated their effort by consecrating the Protestant-republican ideology as both a "social mandate" and a national mission. Early 20th century reformers worked within the earlier common-school tradition while engineering an organizational "revolution" so as to reconfigure the established American *paideia* for an industrial, corporate capital nation-state.[243]

---

[243] David Tyack and Elisabeth Hansot, "From Social Movement to Professional Management: An Inquiry into the Changing Character of Leadership in Public Education," *American Journal of Education* 88 (May 1980): 291-319.

Tyack and Hansot later expanded "From Social Movement to Professional Management" into a book on the same topic. In *Managers of Virtue: Public School Leadership in America, 1820 – 1980* (1982), Tyack and Hansot re-examined the 19th century common school movement that created the U.S. educational system. In structuring their conceptual framework, Tyack and Hansot incorporated much of the "radical critique" of public schooling that historians had written since the late 1960s.[244] Tyack and Hansot argued that 19th century common school reformers saw their educational program as part of a larger mission of consolidating and consecrating a "Christian nation" based on "patriotism, godliness, and prosperity." The project of American nationalism converged with the reformer's visions of the Kingdom of God, whereby, an idealized version of the republic demanded righteous citizens engaged in a providential project. Common school reformers rarely acknowledged their own socio-cultural "blinders" and pontificated as if they spoke for all Americans, thereby, programmatically trying to assimilate citizens and immigrants alike into a chauvinistic WASP "version of Americanism." In the words of one enthusiastic commentator: "American is Protestantism…Protestantism is Life, is Light, is Civilization, is the spirit of the age. Education with all its adjuncts, is Protestantism. In fact Protestantism is education itself." Tyack and Hansot argued that the American common school movement was the "most ambitious and successful social movement" of the 19th century. By century's end, it was able to create "more schooling for more people than in any other nation and resulted in patterns of education that were remarkably uniform in purpose, structure, and curriculum, despite the reality of local control in hundreds of thousands of separate communities."[245]

---

[244] David Tyack and Elisabeth Hansot, *Managers of Virtue: Public School Leadership in America, 1820 – 1980* (New York: Basic Books, 1982). Tyack and Hansot wrote, "Many people (ourselves included) have become newly aware, thanks to the radical analysis, of ideological frameworks and class interests too much taken for granted." They mention in particular Michael B. Katz, *The Irony of Early School Reform: Educational Innovation in Mid-Nineteenth Century Massachusetts* (Cambridge: Harvard University Press, 1968). In summarizing the "radical historians" Tyack and Hansot wrote: "They have sought to demystify public education, to scatter the fog of sentiment that covered harsh realities. They have argued that its basic structure was hierarchical and elitist, not democratic; that its operation was class-biased, racist, and sexist; that it was imposed by elites, not created democratically by educational statesmen and their allies; that its ideology was suffused with notions of social control, often covert; that tinkering with minor improvements would not set it right; and that, most important, its claim of being able to right the basic inequities of American life was a legend" (9).

[245] Ibid., 5, 17, 21-22, 73-76.

Progressive reformers around the turn of the 20th century carried on similar activities, but with a slightly different focus. They sustained the "earlier moral earnestness and sense of mission" of the common school reformers, although Progressives lost "much of the specifically religious content" for a more secular nationalism. Progressives sought to "control the course of human evolution scientifically through improving education." Progressives used a rhetoric of "moral charisma and millennial hope" to sanctify their "dream" of "professionalism" and "social efficiency." Believing whole-heartedly in the "myth" of progress, Progressives saw themselves as "social engineers who sought to bring about a smoothly meshing corporate society," and thereby, "redesign" the public schools to compliment this project. Of course this meant "constraining" public oversight in the schooling process so that public education could become a "professionalized" endeavor that prepared students for their subordinate places in the emerging, modern mass-industrial society.[246]

Tyack and Hansot described administrative Progressives as part of a self-conscious leadership elite (several prominent administrative Progressives described their select group as the "educational trust"). They saw themselves as "professional managers" who were able to reshape the public school system "according to cannons of business efficiency and scientific expertise." These administrative Progressives used a rhetoric of "science and business efficiency" in order to reshape the discourse of public schooling in terms of "problems to be solved by experts." They believed that "experts would run everything to everyone's benefit." This rhetoric helped legitimize institutional reforms whereby educational power was "consolidated" in "large and centralized organizations" that were modeled after corporate structures: "In seeking to depoliticize education, in moving the regulation of education upward and inward in urban and state bureaucracies, in basing legitimation for new authority on scientific expertise, the new managers in education were following patterns of action and thought pioneered in the corporate sector of business." And while the schools were operating more and more like corporate organizations, they were also legitimizing the gross inequality and hierarchy of an industrial mass-society under the cover of a meritocratic equality of opportunity that was supposedly being taught in the public schools. But Tyack and Hansot make clear that the administrative Progressives were contested at every turn and their vision of public schooling was not the only administrative program. However, "the ideology of depoliticized expertise splintered opposition and defused the effectiveness of protest" and thus the "ideology of professionalism"

---

[246] Ibid., 3-8.

was able to entrench the vision and program of administrative Progressives within the centralized, bureaucratic public school system that remains to this day.[247]

In later work, David Tyack and Elisabeth Hansot, along with Robert Lowe, researched Progressive education during the Great Depression in *Public Schools in Hard Time: The Great Depression and Recent Years* (1984). Their emphasis fell on the "complex interaction" of the "political economy of public education" during the Great Depression years and, specifically, how the process and organization of schooling was effected by the tug and pull of "local governance and finance, of growing assertions of state power, and of national influence of various kinds exerted largely through powerful private organizations." They demonstrated how "pluralistic patterns of interests and power" orchestrated "quite different results in different places." Tyack et. al. also discussed the 1930's as the possible "high point" of Progressive education, but acknowledged that different historians have used the "foggy concept" to refer to "many different ideas and practices" so its quite hard to make an argument for its peak.

The conceptual muddle of "Progressivism" was not helped by the reformers penchant for negative ideological maneuvering (what they were against) instead of positive programmatic statements (what they were for). There was also the added difficulty of distinguishing between "what leaders said" and "what actually happened behind the schoolhouse door." The authors noted that Progressive education as a historical concept refers to many "kinds of reformers" who "thought of themselves as Progressive," who defined the significance of "Progressive" in many different ways, and who worked for organizational and curricular modification to meet the needs of changing historical circumstances as they saw it. Social Reconstructionists, reformist administrators, libertarians, and liberals all had a different vision and program of Progressive education. To the extent that "Progressive" reforms in education happened during the Great Depression, it was most significantly a "classroom affair, a new kind of interaction between the teacher and the students," most likely highly varied between different classrooms, schools, and districts, but also limited in terms of the power of tradition teaching practice and cutbacks due to fiscal retrenchment.

---

[247] Ibid., 106-111, 206, 226. David Tyack and Thomas Timar reiterate much of this argument in their brief for the National Commission on Governing America's Schools, "The Invisible Hand of Ideology: Perspectives from the History of School Governance," *Education Commission of the States* (Jan 1999): 1-23.

The authors also noted that as specific cultural and historical contexts dictated, "Progressive methods could be used to serve conservative ends," specifically they mention how "Progressive" reforms rarely if even confronted the structural inequalities associated with race and class. The black school reformer and Progressive Horace Mann Bond articulated this issue clearly at the time (he has often been left out of most historical discussions of "Progressive" education as have other back school reformers of the period). In "The Curriculum and the Negro Child," Bond wrote: "The schools have never built a new social order, but have always in all times in all lands been the instrument through which social forces were perpetuated." Tyack et. al. maintained that no significant widespread "Progressive" changes occurred during the Great Depression years. The organizational and curricular operations of public schools "changed very little," and to the extent there were reforms initiated, the can be seen as "short-term dislocations" in the midst of "long-term continuity."[248]

Outside of the preeminent work of the two leading History of Education scholars, Lawrence Cremin and David Tyack, there have been many other important works published on both Progressive education history and the larger history of educational reform that surrounds this particular movement. One important early work was by C. A. Bowers in 1969, *The Progressive Educator and the Depression: The Radical Years*. Bowers argued that there were two factions within the Progressive educational movement. The more powerful and mainstream faction represented a romantically oriented "cult of the child" and they articulated a child-centered pedagogy. The other faction came to be known as the "Social Reconstructionists." They wanted the schools to be part of a larger effort to address current social problems so as to use the schools to reform society. The Social Reconstructionists used the rhetoric of class struggle to advocate a platform of social planning and socialistic collectivity.

When George S. Counts gave his landmark speech, "Dare Progressive Education Be Progressive?" in 1932, he was both criticizing the movement's political neutrality and urging Progressive educators, specifically members of the PEA, to forsake moderate liberal reformism in order to embrace more radical educational, social and political pieties. Counts of course meant the rejection of capitalism so that schools could embrace and propagate socialism. To further this mission, Counts wanted

---

[248] David Tyack, Robert Lowe, and Elisabeth Hansot, *Public Schools in Hard Times: The Great Depression and Recent Years* (Cambridge, MA: Harvard University Press, 1984): 56-57, 91, 150, 162-63, 180, 189-90.

teachers to become political actors inside the nation's classrooms and, thereby, not be afraid to use "indoctrination' to "check and challenge" capitalist dogma. Counts believed that schools would indoctrinate students no matter what and, thus, the question became, in whose interests would the public school curriculum serve?

The Social Reconstructionists had a very definite idea. In a PEA pamphlet drafted by the Committee on Social and Economic Problems, *A Call to the Teachers of the Nation* (1934), they exhorted teachers to reject capitalism and renew American democracy: "[teachers] owe nothing to the present economic system, except to improve it; they owe nothing to any privileged caste, except to strip it of its privileges...a powerful organization, militantly devoted to the building of a better social order and to the fulfillment...of the democratic aspirations of the American people." Bowers called this "one of the most extreme and utopian statements to be made by any group during the depression" – even more so than the 1934 Manifesto of the Communist Party of the U.S.A.[249]

Bowers critiqued the Social Reconstructionists, usually by surveying the criticisms of their contemporaries; Progressive educationalists like John Dewey and Boyd Bode made many trenchant critiques. Bowers noted several. The Social Reconstructionists had an "ubiquitous sense of mission," which harkened back to the evangelical millennialism of the common school reformers; they often espoused a simplistic utopianism; and they had a romantic conception of the "power of education to eradicate the evil in the world." Bowers also called the Social Reconstructionists "poor social analysts" because they "lacked an understanding of the teacher's actual position in society:" "Even though teachers had no real protection from being dismissed arbitrarily by school boards – and they thus possessed neither economic security nor the ability to formulate significant policy – the Social Reconstructionists viewed them as a force capable of directing social change." Bowers argued that these educational radicals took a position too extreme to align themselves with labor and to infatuated with the schools to fit well with the Communists, which made their call for teachers to lead the class struggle

---

[249] C. A. Bowers, *The Progressive Educator and the Depression: The Radical Years* (New York: Random House, 1969): ix-x, 4-5, 15, 20, 41. Bowers noted that the editors of *The Social Frontier* did not agree with Roosevelt's New Deal plan to implant a welfare state within a capitalistic society. The plan was to organize teachers and then participate with the labor movement in larger unionizing efforts, while also giving students in the classroom a "labor orientation" towards the issues of the day. They even warned their readership that there may be violence, in which case, teachers should feel justified that the "onus will fall on the shoulders of those few who cannot gracefully surrender their privileges in the face of a popular decision" (134,140).

seem ridiculous to most observers. Bowers quipped, "the editor's messianic zeal had led them far down the road of absurdity." Alienating themselves from other Progressives and ignored by other radicals, the Social Reconstructionists eventually abandoned their radical socialism. They took a conservative turn during the war, which intensified afterwards. Calls for class war were exchanged for slogans urging the saving of democracy and the fighting of totalitarianism. Ironically, after their journal folded, the more moderate Social Reconstructionists took the field as the most powerful and influential Progressive educators and exerted an important authority over curricular debates in the late 1940s. The message had now become community centered schools, democratic deliberation, democratic cooperation, and fostering "democratic living." This "new doctrine" would have wide and lasting imprint on the American public schools, but would eventually be rhetorically co-opted more conservative forces in the 1950s.[250]

In "Education and Progressivism," Joel Spring argued that "Progressivism" had been used and defined so broadly, specifically Cremin's use of the term in *The Transformation of the School*, that it was "a valueless definition since it literally includes everyone." Spring criticized the "lack of clarity" and "confused picture" that this "vague" and "obscure" term identified. He instead called for a more "sharply defined" conceptual terminology of educational reform based on the particulars of various reformist ideology. Specifically Spring suggested that reformer's visions "of the good life" – the ultimate purposes reformers were trying to produce in changing individuals and society – could be the best way to conceptualize distinct "reform" movements. Spring focused on one example in his article: the movement for "social efficiency."[251]

Herbert M. Kliebard followed Spring's lead in 1986 when he published the 1st of three editions of his very influential book, *The Struggle for the American Curriculum*. Kliebard completely denied the existence of a Progressive educational "movement:"

> The more I studied [Progressive education] the more it seemed to me that the term encompassed such a broad range, not just of different, but of contradictory, ideas on education as to be meaningless. In the end, I came to believe that the term was not only vacuous but mischievous. It was not just the word "Progressive" that I thought was inappropriate but the implication that something deserving a single name existed and that something could be identified and defined if we only tried.

---

[250] Ibid., 48-51, 144, 151, 181, 201-54.
[251] Joel Spring, "Education and Progressivism," *History of Education Quarterly* 10 (Spring 1970): 53-71.

Instead he argued for competing "interest groups" with "distinct" "ideological positions" and "agendas for action." These factions contemporaneously co-existed in often "antagonistic"
ways, each with its own reform agenda, although sometimes they were able to bury differences in order to form "temporary coalitions around a particular reform." During what has been called the Progressive era, these antagonistic factions "struggled for control of the American curriculum" and the 20th century became an educational "battleground." Often these groups were fighting over the core issue of "differing forms of knowledge" legitimating specific cultural values. Kliebard focused on only four interest groups that represented the major educational divisions at the turn of the century. The most powerful was the entrenched "humanist" group and three reform groups challenging the humanist hegemony were the child study movement, the social efficiency movement, and the social meliorists. Outside the fray, yet infused within it, Kliebard uniquely argued, was the towering figure of John Dewey who while not directly allied with any one group, he helped define and critique the perimeters of 20th century educational reform.[252]

Kliebard refined and articulated his epistemological position with regards to the conceptual territory of "Progressivism" in a 1993 "Afterword" to the 2nd edition entitled "The Search for Meaning: Curriculum Conflict in the Context of Status Politics." He claimed that Progressive education was no more than a "mélange of reforms" that have been "lumped together" under a common term. This was due in a large part to Lawrence Cremin's seminal use of the phrase. While Cremin warned against any one definition, he equated it with "the educational phase of American Progressivism writ large." Edward A. Krug's two volumes on the *Shaping of the American High School* prefigured the turn of direction that would occur in the 1970s when the vagueness and vacuity of the phrase "Progressive movement" was questioned (by Filene and Spring among others), ultimately to be rejected and jettisoned by an influential minority within the historical community. In its place came two new epistemological uses. One was a restricted definition of "Progressive" attached to narrower historical entities, like Tyack's use of "administrative Progressives." The other use focused on the "politically and socially regressive nature" of many so called "Progressive" reforms. Kliebard noted tongue in cheek: "We are left with the feeling that much of what went on in the Progressive era was socially and politically, and perhaps even pedagogically, regressive." Thus instead of even using the term "Progressive," historians like Kliebard

---

[252] Herbert M. Kliebard, *The Struggle for the American Curriculum, 1893 – 1958*, 3rd ed. (1986; reprint, New York: RoutledgeFalmer, 2004), xiv, xviii-xix, 1-52.

have instead looked for ideologically distinct social, political, and educational "movements" that are much more clear and distinguishable in their affiliations, goals, programs, and practices – "persons identified with a movement, in other words, see *themselves as sharing common programs* or beliefs." Using this methodology and narrowing the definition of a "movement" ala Peter G. Filene, Kliebard questioned "Progressivism" out of existence: "Once a movement is understood in this way, one can then go on to determine whether the term *Progressive* can legitimately be applied to such a collective, but it is not clear at all that such a collective exists...In short, neither in terms of the coherence of the program for reform nor in its membership nor in its overall ideology can a definition of Progressivism as a social and political movement be articulated."

Instead of using the terminology of Progressivism, Kliebard formulated his own position, which rested on three points. First, Progressivism cannot be defined "in terms of stable attributes." Second, specific ideological subgroups can be identified and their more "consistent and recognizable ideological positions" can be conceptualized. And third, all reform issues could be complicated by reform coalitions that could consist of a blending of various distinct ideological sub-groups. Thus, Kliebard's conception of "Progressive education" was a broadly sweeping "reaction against tradition structures and practices but with multiple ideological positions and programs of reform." This broad "reaction" is composed of distinct and "reasonably coherent subgroups and movements," but in no way do all these pieces "add up to one Progressive education movement." Hence the central term "struggle" in the title of Kliebard's book. The American curriculum was "contested terrain" and "the prize for which the various interest groups competed."[253]

The political scientist Paul E. Peterson wrote *The Politics of School Reform, 1870 – 1940* (1985) in which he used quantitative methods to study three different urban school systems (Atlanta, Chicago, and San Francisco) in an effort to examine the particulars of late 19th and early 20th century educational reform in three unique historical contexts.

---

[253] Herbert M. Kliebard, "Afterword: The Search for Meaning in Progressive Education: Curriculum Conflict in the Context of Status Politics," in *The Struggle for American Curriculum, 1893 – 1958,* 3rd ed. (1993; reprint, New York: RoutledgeFalmer, 2004), 271-92. Kliebard emphasized his point of educational curriculum being a "battleground:" "Whatever else the curriculum may be in terms of what actually gets taught to children, it is also the arena where ideological armies clash over the status of deeply held convictions...The question of whose cultural and moral values will emerge as dominant...the curriculum in any time and place becomes the site of a battleground where the fight is over whose values and beliefs will achieve the legitimation and the respect that acceptance into the national discourse provides."

In an effort to caution against generalizations, Peterson argued, "diverse participants focused on those specific objectives in which they had the greatest stake. Although some related their specific demands to larger views of the good society, their demands were met by counterclaims with alternative visions:" "Each of these groups had their own distinctive sets of interests; no stable alliance among any two of them was able to determine policy choice in all situations; instead, outcomes in particular instances fluctuated as different coalitions came together in an ever-changing series of uneasy alliances." School policy was a constant battle ground between competing factions. In order to gain "legitimacy," Peterson argued, school officials tried to "separate themselves, as institutions, from particular groups and factions:" "No one social group held sufficient economic and political power to dictate the course of school policy. The ultimate winners in such an uncertain contest were, of course, the schools themselves. As organizations, they could only prosper from contests and conflicts among competing interests." It is out of this complex historical environment that the "politics of institutionalization" took place, whereby, urban educational leaders sought "expansion and professionalization" so as to make public schools an "organized system of autonomous power" within politically divided, fiscally strained, and ethnically contentious communities.[254]

Peterson's study paid particular attention to a "threefold system" of social "stratification" in industrial America differentiated by class, status, and political power – especially in relation to the "noticeably inegalitarian" "structure of educational institutions:"[255] education was a class based institution that "declare[ed] one's social worth" and "validat[ed] the status of social groups." Education was "a prize to be won by each social group in order for that group's culture to be affirmed, legitimated, and perpetuated." To the extent the public schooling became an agent of "cultural imperialism," Peterson argued, it did so not by "compulsory instruction" but by "the exclusion of a group from pubic schooling." Peterson criticized the historical argument that 19th century public schools were used to control and train "docile work force." In stead he argued that public school officials "ignored" ethnic immigrants and the poor "until adequate facilities had been extended to the more

---

[254] Paul E. Peterson, *The Politics of School Reform, 1870-1940* (Chicago: The University of Chicago Press, 1985), 4, 15, 22-23, 207. Peterson nicely summarized the complicated notion of reform in this complex environment: "Reformers' policies were as often rejected as approved. When adopted, they were frequently amended; when promulgated, they were not always implemented" (203).

[255] Peterson conceptual included race and ethnicity under the heading of social "status." He explained that although "school politics had become increasingly marked by class conflict in the first decades of this century, questions of race and ethnicity did not instantly disappear. Especially in the South, race relations remained so significant a concern that class issues were never vigorously articulated:" "ethnic conflicts could interrupt a politics of class" (18-19).

favored:" "Instead of insisting on attendance in publicly controlled institutions, they allowed foreigners to go to their own schools. Instead of keeping potential troublemakers under their watchful eyes, the poorest, most outcast segments of the community went uneducated altogether." But as public schools became more and more "open" and "responsive" to changing community needs, the common pattern of school reform in relation to racial minorities was to give "separate" or "inadequate facilities," or to keep them "completely excluded from education."[256]

Peterson argued that "were it not for widespread citizen involvement in politics, it is likely that the status differences in a culturally pluralistic society would have led to systematic repression of minorities." Local organizations, business, and labor involvement where also at work in expanding the school curriculum: politically powerful ethnic minorities were able to get bilingual education, like the Germans in San Francisco and Chicago; business leaders argued for cheap "basic" education and also manual training; and labor wanted both vocational and a diversified liberal arts curriculum. Peterson noted,

> By the end of the century the debate over the purposes of public education was subtly shifted from questions of cultural incorporation and citizenship to those of compatibility with the demands of the labor market. Thus businessmen could attack foreign-language instruction, music, and some forms of manual training as frivolous departures from the fundamental purposes of public education at the same time that they called for additional courses in the practical skills required for growing industrial economies. Working-class and ethnic groups, on the other hand, defended the differentiated curriculum as an essential ingredient of a democratic society. At the same time, these groups sought practical courses that would widen avenues of economic opportunity. School officials, for their part, maneuvered to protect and expand their organization in the context of these changing political pressures.

This diverse political context was also complicated by the clash of ethnic groups in an American environment of "native dominance" by self professed Anglo Saxons. Peterson argued, based on the evidence he found, "schools were uninterested in (or incapable of) systematic ethnic discrimination" in terms of access to classrooms and resource allocation because school officials were mostly concerned with consolidating their institutional autonomy in the face of hostile local party machines –

---

[256] Ibid., 6, 8-9, 12, 21-23.

although he did qualify this statement by acknowledging that quantitative data cannot "address the quality of the educational experience of children from various ethnic groups" where "ethnic discrimination" most likely happened.[257]

But growing acceptance of ethnic diversity within the public school system was not the whole story. At the same time, many schools across the country practiced a systemic exclusion and segregation of specific minority populations. Peterson focused on the institutional treatment of blacks, Japanese and Chinese populations. Peterson's general explanation for segregation and exclusion of particular ethnic minorities in the U.S. was the lack of political power: "If the group could not impose sanctions on elected officials, the schools were content to provide only the legal minimum, ignoring the barrage of pleas and petitions from the minority. In most cases, political resources were difficult to accumulate because racial minorities either were explicitly denied the right to vote or were left out of the dominant political coalitions." After emancipation blacks in the South were eager for education, but during the later 19th century, they were not only educated separately in segregated and overcrowded facilities (often excluding many students because there was not enough room), but those facilities were also "markedly inferior" and school supplies where often lacking. Blacks were also excluded from secondary schools until 1920. But they had a strong desire for schooling and measure of political power, which they were able to use effectively up until 1892 in order to receive "concrete" educational concessions. However, blacks began to be systematically disenfranchised in 1892 when the Jim Crow South initiated the white primary and voter restrictions and, thus, from 1892 until 1940s blacks found it even harder to improve their meager system of segregated education in the South. In Chicago blacks were able to integrate somewhat into the public schools because they were such a small minority, although when the black population increased by the 1920s de facto segregation ensued and their segregated schools suffered in similar ways as did southern black schools.

Because they were such a small minority in San Francisco, blacks were integrated into the public school system in 1875. But the Chinese, constituting about 9% of the population of San Francisco in 1880, were systematically prevented from any public education until 1884 when a lawsuit allowed segregated schooling, which became the norm well into the 20th century. The Japanese students were allowed to attend integrated schools in San Francisco only because of the considerable support of the Japanese government, which used diplomatic

---

[257] Ibid., 6, 53-71, 73-75, 92. Peterson argued that "rather than a long-term pattern of favoritism, we see early discrimination giving way to increasing acceptance of the larger immigrant groups" (91).

149

leverage with President Roosevelt. Peterson emphasized that many minority populations in the U.S. had to first fight for their right to public schooling (which usually resulted in segregated schools), then they had to fight for educational improvements, and finally they had to fight for integration. Minority success in each stage was the result of "changes in their political status" and as minorities "gained their political rights, their rights to public education also came to be recognized:" "Reform was much more – and much less – than a class struggle, and reformers were often much more – and much less – than a class-conscious elite who imposed their interests and values on a resistant working-class majority. Reform was itself as complex, uncertain, and pluralistic as many of the other forces shaping urban schools."[258]

In 1981 William J. Reese published an award winning paper, "'Partisans of the Proletariat': The Socialist Working Class and the Milwaukee Schools, 1890 – 1920," [259] in which he argued that many histories on "Progressivism" and "Progressive education" have focused too much on "new" middle class professionals and, thereby, have ignored other social groups active at the time, like the urban poor, labor groups, and local socialist parties. He argued that "studies written from the top of the educational system down are certainly valuable, though limited in terms of understanding the process of social change in the schools."[260] Reese argued that the poor and laboring classes were not simply "powerless" and therefore "victimized" by an urban elite. He suggested instead that at the local level radical politics and third-party movements had some political success, and that the "Progressive" era was at the same time "the golden age of Socialism and labor radicalism."

Reese examined Milwaukee, which in 1910 was the first city in the U.S. to be politically swept by a socialist party. Reese detailed the diversity of the socialist "working class"[261] and how through a complex

---

[258] Ibid., 95-117.
[259] William J. Reese, "'Partisans of the Proletariat': The Socialist Working Class and the Milwaukee Schools, 1890 – 1920," *History of Education Quarterly*, 21 (Spring 1981): 3-50.
[260] He went on to write: "But what is missing even in recent historiography is an appreciation of the radical politics and third-party movements which periodically swept many cities in the early 1900s; a recognition of how people from many different social classes and ethnic backgrounds once struggled collectively, if for different reasons and with sometimes contrary results, for reforms easily dismissed by some historians today as examples of 'social control'; and a sense of how immigrants and the urban poor themselves shaped the social life of the school and the contours of the past" (5).
[261] Reese argued, "the 'working class' has never been a single, monolithic, or static entity. Since America was populated by individuals with diverse ethnic, religious, and racial backgrounds, several working class populations have always existed simultaneously. It is therefore impossible for a historian to identify a single 'working class' influence on education, for none has ever existed...In Milwaukee, the Socialist working class grew by accretion, increased its ideological sophistication over time, and represented diverse, shifting elements of laboring people" (6).

historical process it became "intertwined" and engaged in a "symbiotic relationship" with non-socialist groups (middle-class women's groups, Progressive civic groups, and other voluntary associations) in order to form coalitions to address specific reform issues. Through the process of reform coalition, these diverse reform groups interacted and influenced each other socially and politically, and while they differed fundamentally on "ultimate ends," they were able to come to some agreement and find common ground on "immediate programs" like adding free lunch programs or playgrounds to the public school. The Progressive education "movement" from the 1890s to the 1920s, Reese argued, was no more than an "amalgamation of different groups of people who had assembled at different points in time in response to the unique circumstances of Milwaukee politics," and when the times changed during WWI and the coalitions fell apart, the "pieces" of the movement "could not be pieced together again."

Reese and Kenneth Teitelbaum revisited socialist educational reformers in another article a few years later, "American Socialist Pedagogy and Experimentation in the Progressive Era: The Socialist Sunday School" (1983).[262] In this article Reese and Teitelbaum emphasized the socialist commitment to education. They noted that while socialist groups and parties did align in political coalitions with "liberal Progressives and other radicals" over public school reform issues, they also had strong educational initiatives of their own, like the international Socialist Sunday school movement. These schools sought in most causes to supplement the public school education of working class children by teaching them democracy, "the socialist spirit," and "cooperative effort," so as to instill in them the socialist cause and hopefully produce "good rebels." The authors argued for a more diverse understanding of educational reforms during the Progressive era and claimed that the "significance of the Socialist Sunday schools lies in their very existence" as a "dynamic opposition movement to the public school influences of the day."

Reese expanded these early efforts on socialistic reform groups and published his important study, *Power and the Promise of School Reform: Grassroots Movements During the Progressive Era* (1986). In this book Reese focused on the diversity of school reformers during the Progressive era and argued that school reform was "a battleground between various contending interests." School reform was such a contentious issue because a "single system of schools tried to serve a plurality of competing interests." Reese's study looked at the "social

---

[262] Kenneth Teitelbaum and William J. Reese, "American Socialist Pedagogy and Experimentation in the Progressive Era: Te Socialist Sunday School," *History of Education Quarterly* 23 (Winter 1983): 429-454.

conflict" and partisan wrangling over specific educational reforms in Rochester, Toledo, Milwaukee, and Kansas City. He emphasized how actual reforms came into being through the "interaction between many competing forces:" "school innovation and reform were produced by interaction, resistance, adaptation, and accommodation, with the power of capital clearly in a dominant though never unchallenged position."[263]

Reese noted that many prominent middle class, professional, and business elites regarded the public schools as the foundation of a stable social and economic order, and also, as a reporter for the Kansas City's Democratic *Times* claimed, the "handmaiden of economic growth." But the rising control and centralization by urban elites was contested at every turn by many grassroots organizations.[264] Reese called this process a "dialectics of school reform." There was a "constant exchange," Reese argued, between "those who would centralize and those who would decentralize power." There was also cooperation as "shifting coalitions" would come together temporarily on different issues to campaign for municipal reform. Reese noted one issue in particular that was popular and was able to unite various ideological groups: the overall expansion of the social functions of public schooling, like playgrounds, lunches, and medical care. But with the coming of WWI the "spirit of civic activism" collapsed and the community became polarized, thus undermining "faith in cooperation" and bringing to an end the "remarkable era of grassroots Progressivism."[265]

The black historian and Progressive Horace Mann Bond published "Education in the South" in 1939. In this article he agreed with the unabashed fascist Lawrence Dennis that schools were often the "instrument of a dominant elite" and that these elites have used education as a form of "social control." While he criticized Dennis, Bond criticized American education even more when he wrote: "The concept of social forces has not been neglected in application to educational institutions in America as a whole." But Bond emphasized the South where the "dominant planting aristocracy" has used public schools "to maintain both the structure of social classes and that of racial caste" in order to protect their economic and social interests. Bond noted that "the masses of white people in Southern States have, slowly and grudgingly, fought

---

[263] William J. Reese, *Power and the Promise of School Reform* (1986; reprint, New York: Teachers College Press, 2002), 1-2, 123, 130, 213-14.
[264] Reese characterized these grassroots reformers as a "multidimensional political movement:" "A variety of motivation, perceptions, personalities, and interests converged in the making of grassroots Progressivism … Grassroots Progressivism, therefore, had its middle-class and feminine as well as working-class and Socialist roots, growing together in the 1890s like entangling vines that crossed but did not always join. The Social Gospel and Progressive religion added the final stimulus to the growth of municipal reform" (123, 70).
[265] Ibid., 9, 70, 80-81, 118, 121-23, 133, 214, 222-226.

toward the achievement of systems of universal education for white children," but blacks were left largely outside the push for reform. Bond ended his article by saying that black education may improve, but as long as the "determination of control" lay with powerful, white, racist elites, "we may expect to flow inevitably educational structures that are the instruments of the dominant social and economic class which creates and controls them."[266]

Taking a page from Bond, James D. Anderson published an important addition to the Progressive education literature, although it was not really about Progressive education. It was rather an indictment of the educational establishment, which failed to enact truly "Progressive" reforms as far as the second-class education of blacks in South was concerned. In *The Education of Blacks in the South, 1860 – 1935* (1988), Anderson argued for a new understanding of American education in relation to its tortured history with African Americans:

> It is crucial…to recognize that within American democracy there have been classes of oppressed people and that there have been essential relationships between popular education and the politics of oppression. Both schooling for democratic citizenship and schooling for second class citizenship have been basic traditions in American education…Black education developed within this context of political and economic oppression.

Anderson made it clear that during the late 19th and early 20th centuries both Northern and Southern whites were in many ways "white supremacists" and "insisted on a second-class education" for blacks in order to accommodate them for "subordinate roles in the southern economy."[267]

Anderson argued that in black educational circles Book T. Washington stood virtually alone in pandering to white gradualism by developing the Hampton-Tuskegee Idea which offered only industrial education. Most black educators, black families, and black students wanted a liberal arts style education, just like the majority of white students received. In regards to education, and much else, Anderson characterized blacks as a "responsible and politically self-conscious social class." But due to their subordinate and disenfranchised position, blacks were largely unable to get what they wanted educationally (not to mention politically). Both white Southern educationalists and Northern

---

[266] Horace Mann Bond, "Education in the South," *Journal of Educational Sociology* 12 (Jan 1939): 264-74.
[267] James D. Anderson, *The Education of Blacks in the South, 1860 – 1935* (Chapel Hill, NC: The University of North Carolina Press, 1988), 1-2, 279.

educational philanthropists shared a certain "unity of belief in white supremacy," which largely restricted (and sometimes outright forced) the channels of black education into segregated, inferior, and mostly industrial education. Many white Southerners felt that school was "inappropriate" for blacks because "learning will spoil the nigger for work." Those white Southerners who conceded the need for black education wanted an educational system that would properly control blacks so as to keep them a permanent class of exploited labor. Northern white missionaries and philanthropists were infused by a combination of white supremacy, paternalism, and democratic idealism. They wanted blacks to have the Hampton/Tuskeegee model of education so that blacks would become skilled, secure and satisfied in their position as exploited labor. Not surprisingly the Hampton/Tuskeegee model of education often resembled slave labor with the "educational" curriculum consisting of 10-11 hours of agricultural work a day (for 6-7 days a week) supplemented with some evening classes for the more intellectually gifted. Anderson concluded his study by focusing on the frustrated struggle of blacks for educational opportunity: "The education of blacks in the South reveals that various contending forces sought either to repress the development of black education or to shape it in ways that contradicted black's interests in intellectual development. The educational outcomes demonstrate that blacks go some but not much of what they wanted. They entered emancipation with fairly definite ideas about how to integrate education into their broader struggle for freedom and prosperity, but they were largely unable to shape their future in accordance with their social vision."[268]

In the late 1970s and early 80s Ronald K. Goodenow wrote a series of articles dealing with Progressive education and questions of race and ethnicity. In these articles he made clear that "Progressivism" is a "complex and shifting phenomenon" that "defies easy definition" and thus he warned that historical "over-generalization is dangerous"[269] We will be looking at two of his papers that dealt with the broader themes of Progressivism covered in this essay.

---

[268] Ibid., 13, 15, 20-21 67, 92, 285.
[269] Ronald K. Goodenow, "The Progressive Educator, Race and Ethnicity in the Depression Years: An Overview," *History of Education Quarterly* 15 (Winter 1975): 365-94; "The Progressive Educator on Race, Ethnicity, Creativity, and Planning: Harold Rugg in the 1930s," *Review Journal of Philosophy and Social Science* 1 (Winter 1977): 105-28; "The Progressive Educator as Radical or Conservative: George S. Counts and Race," *History of Education Quarterly* 17 (Winter 1977): 45-57; "Racial and Ethnic Tolerance in John Dewey's Educational and Social Thought: The Depression Years," *Educational Theory* 26 (Winter 1977): 48-64; "The Paradox in Progressive Educational Reform: The South and the Education of Blacks in the Depression Years," *Phylon* 39 (March 1978): 49-65; "The Southern Progressive Educator on Race and Pluralism: The Case of William Heard Kilpatrick," *History of Education Quarterly* 21 (Summer 1981): 147-70.

His article, "The Progressive Educator, Race and Ethnicity in the Depression Years: An Overview," dealt with two scholarly omissions in the historical literature on the Progressive era. Few historians had scrutinized the views of white Progressive educators on race and ethnicity, and few had looked at the "contribution of blacks and ethnics to Progressive education." Goodenow noted that some members of the PEA and many social reconstructionists did discuss racial discrimination and attempt to theorize ethnic conflict, although they generally organized their views around an assimilationist/Americanization framework. Goodenow argued that there were two basic positions that Progressive educators took: "social-structural and institutional" determinants of racial discrimination (Dewey, Counts, Mabel Carney, and Buell Gallagher), and "cultural and psychological" causes of racial prejudice (Kilpatrick and Rugg). The PEA as an organization discussed race and ethnicity within the confines of the Commission on Intercultural Education (1936-38), but the initiatives of this commission generally ignored structural-institutional determinants of racism and ended up stressing a depoliticized "cultural contribution" approach in an effort to promote national unity, tolerance, and democracy.

This article also looked at Southern Progressivism, which as an educational program was mostly concerned with the "modernization" of Southern schools, i.e. standardized curriculum, teacher professionalization, and centralized control of schools. Outside of a few notable exceptions (Mabel Carney and Buell Gallagher), there was little effort done to address race in the South except of course to reinforce segregationist and paternalist social control. One Southern state curriculum guide explicitly stated that blacks were "a constant menace to the health of the community, a constant threat to its peace and security, and a constant cause of and excuse for the retarded progress of the other race." Despite the pious and often empty rhetoric of white reformers, which could serve conservative as well as Progressive ends, blacks were highly interested in Progressivism and generally saw "considerable potential" in using Progressive-democratic rhetoric to their advantage. By turning Progressive rhetoric against white moderates it became "more difficult for them openly to oppose democratic change." There were also liberal black critics of Progressivism, like Horace Mann Bond, who criticized most Progressive programs for not addressing the structural-institutional determinants of racial oppression and for assuming that a "democratic social order" existed in which blacks could democratically seek to address their grievances and fulfill their aspirations.

Goodenow revisited Southern Progressivism three years later in "Paradox in Progressive Educational Reform: The South and the Education of Blacks in the Depression Years." Goodenow argued that Southern Progressivism was concentrated on "modernization while concurrently maintaining fundamentally racist patters that themselves were contradictory to much Progressive ideology." The main programmatic efforts of Southern Progressives addressed standardized curriculum, scientific management, teacher professionalization, and centralized state control. Within these programs "tolerance" was often used as a rhetoric for segregation and social control. Blacks were to be trained "for loyalty, essentially menial tasks, and continued segregation." Goodenow condemned much of the Progressive program and its democratic rhetoric as "[Booker T.] Washington's accommodationism in modern garb." The PEA as an organization generally avoided the race issue, but several of its members confronted radical discrimination either directly (Counts, Dewey, Mabel Carney, and Buell Gallagher) or in more oblique ways (Kilpatrick).

Goodenow also claimed that "historians of Progressivism have totally ignored" the literature of black Progressives like W. A. Robinson, Doxey Wilkerson, Alain Locke, Charles Johnson, and Horace Mann Bond.[270] Some black Progressives used Progressive rhetoric and methods for consciousness raising and social change. Others, like Bond, argued that Progressive educational reform was futile unless the institutional structure of segregation and racism was attacked: "Let us confess that the schools have never built a new social order, but have always in all times in all lands been the instruments through which social forces were perpetuated." In a racist society ruled by racist "social forces," Bond argued, all educational reform, whatever the rhetoric, would be structured in favor of whites. In summary, Goodenow condemned Progressivism in the South as a form of "social control," while he praised it in its role of offering "opportunity to create a more democratic social conscience among whites and a heightened demand for justice among blacks." He also praised black Progressives like Bond who criticized and exposed the paradoxes of Progressivism by "testing its democratic ideology against real conditions of oppression."

---

[270] Historians of the Progressive era and Progressive education began to take more concerted note of ethnic minorities by the 1970s. David Tyack for one has devoted much space to ethnic minorities, including blacks, within many of his educational histories. Ronald E. Butchart has traced the rich historiography of African American education, and expertly categorized and analyzed the subject up until the late 1980s. Ronald E. Butchart, "'Outthinking and Outflanking the Owners of the World": A Historiography of the African American Struggle for Education," *History of Education Quarterly* 28 (Autumn 1988): 333-66.

By 1992 the debate on Progressive education had come full circle and Mustafa Emirbayer was basically fleshing out and expanding Lawrence Cremin's original position. In "Beyond Structuralism and Voluntarism: The Politics and Discourse of Progressive School Reform, 1890 – 1930"[271] Emirbayer started with Cremin's landmark conception of the Progressive education as "the educational phase of American Progressivism writ large," and re-proposed a monolithic interpretation on this movement. He seemingly defined educational Progressives in a very general way: "inspired by Dewey's vision, a wide range of educators, parents, and community leaders came together during the late nineteenth and early twentieth centuries in an impassioned crusade to transform American public schooling." With this definition he overlooked or ignored pluralistic arguments that denied a monolithic movement and, despite his claim for an empirical foundation, his sociological and political science framework drive an overly deterministic conception that often resulted in superficial and simplistic analysis.[272] He also based his conceptual framework on one historical context, Boston, and claimed that "school reform unfolded in not dissimilar ways in many other school systems across the county," although he does admit that his "generalizations" do not "extend as readily to the South." Despite these serious failings, his overall analytical framework is intriguing and is very similar to the overall conclusion that I will be drawing at the end of this essay, so his argument merits a closer look.

Emirbayer put forth a conception of Progressivism as "discursive acts[273] by state-building elites," and he situated his concept within a critical synthesis of two general trends that he found "inadequate." He critiqued the strengths and weaknesses of both the school of "structuralist" analysis (Bowles and Gintis, Katz, Nasaw, and

---

[271] Mustafa Emirbayer, "Beyond Structuralism and Voluntarism: The Politics and Discourse of Progressive School Reform, 1890 – 1930," *Theory and Society* 21 (Oct 1992): 621-64.

[272] Emirbayer often made statements or used the pronoun "they" to refer to "Progressives" and then made generalizations that are highly suspect, given that not all "Progressives" would have agreed with or argued for a particular position. For instance, he claimed "they proposed the reorganization of classroom instruction so that it would promote each student's capacities for social interaction and creative problem-solving" (625). For a more complicated conception of "Progressive" education see Kliebard, *The Struggle for the American Curriculum*. Since Emirbayer claimed that "educational research has neglected the microscopic domain of curriculum and pedagogy," it is curious that he did not find, read, or reference Kliebard's groundbreaking book. Even the conservative Diane Ravitch referenced Kliebard in her summary book on the subject, *Left Back: A Century of Battles Over School Reform* (New York: Touchstone, 2000), 33, 54, 529. The omission of Kliebard is also troubling given the close similarity between Emirbayer's "struggle" thesis and Kliebard's conception of curricular "struggle."

[273] Emirbayer agued that Progressive "discourse" was a "major element behind the transformation of public school systems and of moral and civic education:" "to formulate precisely such a discourse, to refashion old symbols, images, and ideals into a new agenda for redeeming the unfulfilled promise of American education." See also Daniel T. Rogers, "In Search of Progressivism."

Peterson) and also the school of "cultural" analysis (Cremin, Kaestle, Tyack and Hansot). He argued that structural analysis over-determined institutional power at the expense of human actors, it failed to account for the historical timing of Progressive reforms, and it neglected the importance of cultural factors. He also argued that cultural analysis tended to "err in the direction of one-sided voluntarism" and ignore "objective constraints on voluntaristic action."

Emirbayer broke the Progressive education movement down into three contexts: curricular and pedagogical reforms at the local and national levels; local initiatives to reform the political and administrative structure of schools; and the professionalization of teaching and administrative, including organizational building. He claimed that "each of these diverse streams of educational Progressivism manifests its own distinctive rhythm and trajectory. But we can nonetheless group them all together under a common banner because...they all shared a common, unifying discourse, a similar set of concerns expressed in the ideals and images of civic republicanism, Protestant millennialism and liberal individualism." Progressives used very influential "cultural discourses" to unite disparate groups into a "broad-based coalition" to achieve the "larger goal" of creating "a new moral basis for American society." Emirbayer noted that Progressive education reforms "long outlasted" other reform movements of the Progressive era because of a unique "agenda." Progressive education debates represented discursive "struggles" of "oppositional and dominant groups" that battled over different visions and legitimations of the "sacred center" of the "public sphere." Both "administrative" and "pedagogical" Progressives were "driven by" a "state-building ideology," which infused their moral crusade for a corporate welfare state that they envisioned would unite a fragmented urban-industrial republic. Progressive educators and administrators were working towards a "new moral order" to check the "corruption" and "decay" of older social institutions so as to preserve and consecrate some type of "normative order" at the "sacred center" of American society:

> In their optimistic view, educational reform would help to redeem commonly shared American values and bring ever closer to reality the new "democratic" society that was the true American destiny...As "the educational phase of American Progressivism writ large," the discourse of the Progressive school reformers embodied both the "social control" dimension so typical of Progressive rhetoric in general, and its more hopeful and millennialist aspiration to a new "national community"...school reformers envisioned a generalized Christian spirituality as the basis for an "intentionally progressive" democracy striving toward ever "more perfect union."

The actualization of the Progressive educational reform was often an "Americanization" program of "socialization" intended for both native and immigrant students. The socialization process of the curriculum also included differentiation and tracking so as reinforce class-based structures of the American economy. The end result of these reforms was "often profoundly undemocratic" and "culturally oppressive. Emirbayer gave Progressive educational reformers credit for being successful in "forging a broad-based coalition" around their distinctive "vision," which far outlasted all other Progressive reform initiatives and helped usher in a measure of "social stability" over the course of the 20th century.

Before we conclude this essay, we will look at two recent articles that have placed Progressive education within an international context and therefore complicate any conceptual usage of the term. Marjorie Lamberti studied Progressive education in Imperial Germany at the turn of the century in "Radical Schoolteachers and the Origins of the Progressive Education Movement in Germany, 1900-1914."[274] Lamberti chronicles the rise of the *neue Padagogik* (new pedagogy) and the *Arbeitsschule* (child-centered school) through the efforts of two predominant strains of Progressive reformers in Germany: radical reformers in Bremen and Hamburg, and more moderate Progressives in Saxony. Both schools of thought combined a critique of religious instruction in the schools (they wanted it more in line with Modernist scholarship, but not eliminated – although some of the radicals wanted it eliminated) and they put forward a broader critique of teaching practices that were teacher centered, fact oriented, and not in line with the new research in psychology. These Progressives drew upon German strains of Progressive pedagogy, German culture, and the new research in psychology at German universities, but several influential leaders had also been influenced by John Dewey's work, especially *The School and Society* (1899). The more moderate and majority of German Progressives focused on child centered and learning-by-doing pedagogy that tailored curriculum and instruction to the developmental and psychological needs of the child, while also increasing the professionalization and autonomy of teachers as child development experts. Although Progressives represented a minority of German teachers, they had a deep impact on the profession and were able to convince the German Teachers' Association to adopt the "new pedagogy" during the national congress in May 1912, whereby active-learning was added to this organizations program of reform. This was seven years before the American Progressive Education Association was even founded.

---

[274] Marjorie Lamberti, "Radical Schoolteachers and the Origins of the Progressive Education Movement in Germany, 1900 -1914," *History of Education Quarterly* 40 (Spring 2000): 22-48.

Jurgen Herbst reviewed the English translation of a German handbook, which centered on the international context of Progressive education.[275] The book lacked a clear focus and covered several somewhat successful European Progressive educators and educational movements as well as some less successful attempts in other parts of the globe. In pondering the international aspect of Progressive education and the editor's conceptual befuddlement, Herbst rhetorically raised the question of "how far we want to extend the circle that includes activities we might want to classify under progressive education." "Are there no viable criteria of inclusion and exclusion? Does everything fit?" Herbst analyzed this question by way of a chapter on the development of progressive education in Europe by Jurgen Oelkers. Herbst summarized that ever since the Reformation "academic institutions were run by governmental authorities in the interest and for the benefit of the state," and thus European *Reformpadagogik* had existed alongside the state in "symbiotic relationship" as a "continuous structure" of counter-pedagogical practice stressing "the individualistic spirit" in "antagonistic" relation with the standardization of nationalism. This suggests that since the Reformation Progressive education has been a social institution that has vied with nationalists over competing visions of the public sphere contained within the centralized organization of the state. In light of this conceptualization Herbst asked, "it may well be time now to ask whether there is such a thing as a theory of progressive education and, if there is, whether we should begin to debate and define it."

To conclude this discussion of Progressive education it would be helpful to first restate the conclusions of the last chapter. It is clear that there were many reformist groups of various political and ideological stripes at the turn of the 20th century, of which Progressivism was but one example. As a culturally homogeneous and economically secure social class (although uneasy in their security), Progressive reformers had the ability, education, and socio-economic resources to create many diverse voluntary organizations, including educational organizations, which they used to further various social, economic, political, and cultural causes. Progressives were animated on the whole by a Republican-Populist-Protestant infused ideological orientation that often blended capitalist, scientific, and professional methods, all under a politicized and racialized banner of WASP "Americanism."

---

[275] Jurgen Herbst, review of *Progressive Education Across the Continents: A Handbook*, ed. Hermann Rohrs and Volker Lenhart, *History of Education Quarterly* 37 (Spring 1997): 45-59.

Progressives sought many types of social change and aligned themselves with various other ideological groups to achieve reform coalitions on specific issues and initiatives, but they were primarily concerned with devising a clear and efficient *order* to harness modernity and industrialization under the tri-partite *control* of 1) a regulatory State integrated with 2) WASP civic associations and business corporations, and directed by 3) a technocratic elite. "Americanization" as a nationalistic and cultural identity was the *new order* the Progressives sought.

The Progressive educational "movement," to the extent that one can call it a movement outside of the organizational activities of PEA members and their associates, was most explicitly a general educational trend towards a more humane and child centered pedagogy often couched in the language of socialization and democracy – a general educational trend that was spreading across Europe as well. But Progressive education in the U.S. was also a cultural movement that sought to define a WASP America in its own ideology[276] and interests and, thereby, to socialize and acculturate American minorities into the dominant Anglo culture (to the extent that different minority groups were deemed worthy of acculturation in specific geographical contexts). Many minorities were deliberately excluded from Americanization or were offered inclusion on very demeaning, second-class terms. However, more liberal and radical strands of the Progressive movement, especially within its educational manifestations, articulated a more inclusive, community oriented, democratic, tolerant, and multicultural dimension to the Americanization program.

Although often in paternalistic, class-based, and racist language, these more liberal rhetorics of Americanization offered up democratic ideals that inspired minority populations to challenge the rhetorical Progressive platitudes of freedom, equality, and justice against the tarnished realities of the status quo. And arguably as minority populations mobilized, minority leaderships organized, and civil demonstrations multiplied, the more liberal Progressives began to modify their conceptions of the WASP Americanization program and replace it with a more inclusive and multicultural conception – so much so that over

---

[276] Carl F. Kaestle, "Ideology and American Educational History," *History of Education Quarterly* 22 (Summer 1982): 123-37. Kaestle defined the progressive ideology as a "moral culture based on Anglo-American Protestantism, republicanism, and capitalism" that asserted "centralist, assimilationist, and moralistic" values and "cultural preferences." He called progressive reformers "hegemonic" because "they were didactic and ethnocentric" and tried to "promote publicly" their cultural value system through public education (128, 130).

the course of the 20th century the liberal state's executive, legislative, and judicial branches would actually articulate and consecrate the civil rights of *all* Americans for the first time in the nation's history. Of course the more liberal Progressive rhetoric and the rising mobilization of minorities was countered and contested by a more conservative majority, and thus ensued over the course of the 20th century and into the 21st century a *struggle* – a cultural war – not only for the American *paideia*, but for the very meaning and "sacred center" of America. The Progressive Americanization movement is an unfinished project that defines the parameters of the 21st century, which as I write is still the outline of a contested battlefield, and education, as always, is at the center of the political struggle to define the cultural conception of a nation. At the heart of the conflict is a WASP culture that is loosing *control* – loosing the ability to exclusively define and delineate the *moral order* that is supposed to unite a nation. The roots of this conflict lie at the foundation of the Progressive era. The early 20th century Progressive movement, to the extent that there was a unified movement, embraced many offensive strategies to protect and preserve their WASP culture: discrimination, segregation, centralization, corporatization, and above all else public and private programs of "Americanization."

About the Author

Beach is a lecturer at the University of Texas, San Antonio. He has advanced degrees in English, History, Philosophy, and Education.

Beach has been a teacher and educational administrator for over fifteen years, teaching an array of subjects to a broad range of students, from pre-school all the way to high school, in public and private schools, in the U.S. and in South Korea. Previously Beach was a Lecturer at Oregon State University, the University of California, and at several community colleges in Southern California and Central Texas.

Beach's scholarly research includes Studies in Poetry: The Visionary (2004), Studies in Ideology: Essays on Culture and Subjectivity (2005), Gateway to Opportunity? A History of the Community College in the United States (2011), and Children Dying Inside: A Critical Analysis of Education in South Korea (2011). Beach has also written a textbook, Educating for Democracy (2008).

Beach has published five volumes of poetry, including his volume of selected poems, Living into Words: Poetry in a Time of Killing (2007).

Links to his books, articles, conference papers, and poetry can be found at his website at www.jmbeach.com

www.ingramcontent.com/pod-product-compliance
Lightning Source LLC
Chambersburg PA
CBHW061255280526
45784CB00002B/773